OUR NEW OLD ENEMIES

Our New Old Enemies

Stephen A. Reger

STEPHEN REGER BOOKS

Table of Contents

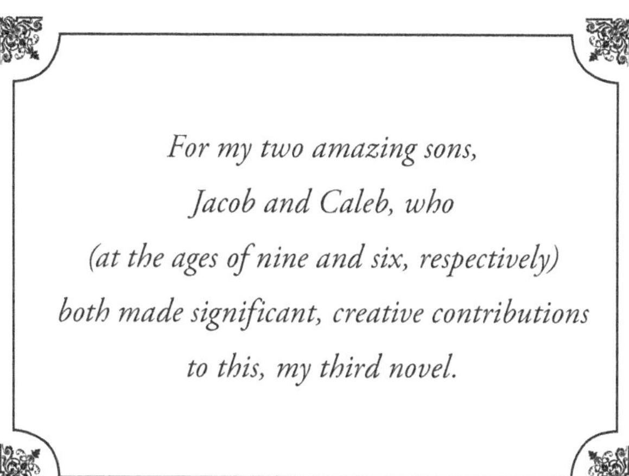

For my two amazing sons,
Jacob and Caleb, who
(at the ages of nine and six, respectively)
both made significant, creative contributions
to this, my third novel.

"If horrible events can be traced to a cabal of evildoers who control the world from behind a vast curtain, that's, in one sense, less scary than the idea that some horrible things happen at random or as a result of a lone, nebbish, a nobody. The existence of a secret cabal means that there's some sort of order in the world; a catastrophic fluke suggests there's a vast crevice of chaos, the essence of dread."

-Fred Kaplan, *Slate* magazine,
November 14, 2013

Part One

Lives of Quiet Desperation

CHAPTER ONE

The quote that "God has a special providence for fools, drunkards, and the United States of America," has often been attributed to Prussian statesman Otto von Bismarck. While it's likely apocryphal, for there is little to no evidence that he ever actually used those words, Bismarck's renowned statement was, at best, incomplete. Cane Canyon was living proof that God also favored lawmen, Poles, and cowboys (but not the kind who played football in Dallas).

Born *Czeslaw Kanion*, this forty-five-year-old FBI agent hated Mondays—almost as much as he hated his job.

But that hadn't always been the case.

Actually, that was not entirely true; he had always hated Mondays. Mondays were to the work week what Mexican fast food was to the body—something to be avoided at all costs, likely as not to give you a raging case of mutant diarrhea.

But Cane hadn't always hated his job.

He was an FBI agent, and that had meant something—once. Once upon a time, when he started with the agency back in 2003, he was an idealistic, twenty-five-year-old law enforcement officer. He did his job well, and he did it with both pride and honor.

But somewhere along the way—he wasn't sure when, but it probably coincided with the promotion of Jed Meadodo to the post of director for the Cincinnati field office of the FBI—his job had changed. Under Meadodo's so-called leadership, and that of the mental midget president who had decided to turn the FBI into his own personal political weapon, his job had switched from being a cop to being a bureaucrat.

As Cane slipped out of bed and lit his breakfast—a Marlboro Red that was certain to be one of at least thirty that this self-styled cowboy would smoke that day—he wondered, and not for the first time, why people were so stupid. How could sixty-three million Americans be dumb enough to elect a narcissistic, millionaire, TV personality with no ability, no credentials and no fucking clue, when dozens of Governors, Senators, former Secretaries of State, and Attorneys General—men and women with impeccable credentials and records of scholarship and achievement—were available? Since when had credentials become a bad thing? When had the term elite become a pejorative? And when had it become *populist* to blindly support rich assholes whose greatest accomplishments were that they were now even richer and bigger assholes?

Was it any wonder then that this thin-skinned, born-with-a-silver-spoon-up-his-ass, carnival barker had appointed the worst government in US history? A CIA Director who likely couldn't spell CIA right, even if given three chances; a Secretary of Education who clearly had no education, other than knowing how to shoot off a rifle with about as much accuracy as she could shoot off her big mouth; a Treasury Secretary who had bankrupted both of the banks dumb enough to have made him a CFO; a corpulent Secretary of Agriculture who had clearly never encountered a vegetable in his life, a Secretary of the Interior who knew about as much about nature as a neurosurgeon knew about building houses; a secretary of Veterans' Affairs who had never served a single day in uniform; a FEMA Director who was assured of job security simply because he was a walking, talking federal disaster area, and an EPA Director who though *climate change* was setting the temperature in his Cadillac Escalade at 72 degrees rather than 71.

And then there was Cane's immediate supervisor. The director of the Cincinnati field office of the FBI—Jed Meadodo. First of all, the fact that his last name was *Me A Dodo* was the truest statement Cane had ever heard. Second, the only thing that he had ever learned from this life-long bureaucrat had been Meadodo's vaunted "Four Pillars of Good Police Work"—cardinal rules of survival in the increasingly political world of law enforcement. Specifically, he had learned:

1. Thou shalt not show initiative of any kind
2. Thou shalt not stand out in any way
3. Thou shalt not volunteer any unsolicited advice
4. Above all, thou shalt not embarrass the boss

And as a first generation American, the son of industrious and hard-scrabble Polish immigrants, that mentality just didn't work for Cane. In fact, very little of the twenty-first century worked for him. He just couldn't understand most people these days. In fact, he often wondered whether Darwin had been wrong all along. Was man still an ape? If not, if man had truly evolved, then how could one explain the enormous number of seemingly *unevolved* people on the planet? Those who thought that Rami Malek and Freddie Mercury were the same person; those who put ketchup on hot dogs instead of mustard; people who actually listened to Justin Bieber; fans of the Dallas Cowboys; people from Florida; and idiots who said shit like, "Working hard, or hardly working?"

In fact, he felt so completely separate from what constituted "the norm" or "mainstream culture" that he often felt like Superman, an alien who had been transplanted to Earth, but who wasn't really one of *us*. Or perhaps he was some modern-day Moses, sent down the river to a strange and exotic culture, far different from his own.

As frustrated as he was by the annoying banality of the so-called "average person," he was even more frustrated by the fact that most everyone he met assumed that he, too, was an ignorant oaf. Much of it, he knew, was due to his size. He was six foot four and weighed nearly three hundred pounds, and while he had very little fat on his rather bulky frame, his bull neck and barrel shaped torso made him look like an ex-NFL lineman or an out of work professional wrestler. In fact, when he was just twelve years old, his father—who had just seen *Dances With Wolves* and had decided to give both Cane and his two brothers "authentic" Native American names—began to refer to him as "Blocks the Sun." Or, perhaps, it was his rather unusual name, the Americanized version of which made him sound like a reject from a Louis L'amour novel. Either way, upon first glance, very few people would believe that Cane Canyon, this larger-than-life monster with the silly name, actually had an IQ of 164 and was fluent in four different languages.

As he downed the day's first cup of coffee and got dressed for work, he thought about something his partner, *Ack Ack* Adamson had said to him just two days ago. As they had gone their separate ways for the weekend, Adamson had said, "You know, Cane, the only thing worse than hating your job is not having one at all."

As he left his small apartment in the chic Over the Rhine section of Cincinnati, Cane wasn't so sure if his partner had been right. After all, *Ack Ack* hated his own family, and he probably wouldn't have subscribed to the idea that the only thing worse than hating your family was not having one at all.

Professional frustrations aside, Cane was spared the tension that went along with having a wife, 2.33 children, a mortgage, a house in the suburbs, and a minivan. A bachelor for life, he was perfectly content to escape each night from the FBI's field office in Kenwood to his small and outrageously overpriced apartment in the most heavily gentrified area of southwest Ohio. It was a safe haven where he would never have to endure the excruciating "How was your day?" conversation at dinner; where he could eat whatever he wanted, whenever he wanted; where he could watch *Goodfellas* or *The Godfather* all the time, every day, without any hint of interruption; and, best of all, where he was not a slave to monogamy.

Or, perhaps, the "best of all" was the fact that he would never have to drive a minivan. *Who was the comedian who once said that any man that drives a minivan doesn't care about life?* he often asked himself.

In any event, as he eased into his gorgeous, two-door, 1968 Mercury Monterey Fastback (a car that he had lovingly christened Laverne and that was roughly the size of a WWII battleship), he extinguished his second cigarette of the morning and keyed the ignition. The sound that the 6.4 liter, Big-Block, V8, 256 horsepower engine made as it came to life was positively therapeutic, borderline erotic; and, for just a moment, his trepidation about spending another day under the "tutelage" of his assclown boss was washed away. But as he eased his vintage monster out into the relatively light early morning traffic on Vine Street and began his trip north to Kenwood, his cellphone began to ring, and he could see that it was his boss calling.

Already.

At 5:30 am.

On a Monday.

And he just knew it was going to be a shitter of a day—one that, perhaps, even Laverne couldn't cure.

CHAPTER TWO

In *Walden*, American transcendentalist writer Henry David Thoreau famously wrote that "the mass of men lead lives of quiet desperation." That statement was never more true than it was of Abell Adamson.

Abell loved Mondays; but that was only because of how much he loved his job—or, more precisely, because of how much he hated his personal life.

Abell (who went by *A.A.; Double A*, or just *Battery*; *Ack Ack*, and any other variation of his initials his low brow co-workers could produce—his least favorite being *Ready, Willing, and Able*) was a married father of three. Like his partner, Cane Canyon, he was forty-five years old, but therein the similarities ended.

His wife, Felicity (*God help anyone who marries a girl with a virtue for a name, like Charity, Chastity, or Serenity*, he often mused) had "gifted" him with the three most entitled girls on the planet—Daisy, Sadie, and Amber (fourteen, twelve, and ten, respectively). Three girls who, for as much as they ever listened to their father, should have been named Ariel, Belle, and Jasmine. Each one of his three "Disney princesses" attended a different private school in Cincinnati—private but not parochial; after all, imagine the horror if anyone of the three should ever be exposed to religion—all so that, as Felicity had explained, each girl could "invent an identity for herself that was uniquely her own."

Whatever the fuck that meant.

And his relationship with his three daughters (four, if you counted Felicity, who liked to think of herself as her daughters' best friend) consisted almost entirely of writing checks to support their lavish spending habits. As a result, rather than living in a palatial Indian Hill estate, they lived in a modest four-bedroom home in the middle-class suburb of Loveland. And rather than driving a 2023 Chevrolet Corvette convertible to work, he spent an hour each day on I-275 and I-71 fighting traffic from inside a beige 1985 Dodge Caravan. But, while a part of him died every day when he got inside the "Beige Bitch," at least he was comforted by the fact that his daughters all had $250 pairs of yoga pants into which they could squeeze their considerable asses—at least that's what Felicity (who, unlike the "Beige Bitch," no longer allowed him to squeeze himself inside of her) told him on a semi-regular basis.

Looking through his meager closet and imagining for just a moment that it was stocked with Cesare Attolini or Edward Sexton suits, he selected a navy-blue disaster that might have been fashionable twenty years ago, back when it had graced the discount rack at someplace like Sears or JC Penney's. *Hell, even a Hugo Boss would be a significant upgrade from this piece of shit*, he mused, as he made his selection. Noticing that the slacks didn't even really correctly match the jacket, he just shrugged his shoulders as if to say, *Who gives a damn? No one's going to look at you anyway. You're wearing the minivan of suits.*

Then, his clothing selection made and Bruce Springsteen's "Dancing in the Dark" pleasantly stuck in his head, he stepped into the bathroom to "check his look in the mirror." And, just like the iconic character in Springsteen's classic song of middle-aged angst, he wanted to "change his clothes, his hair, his face."

He was smallish, bald, and plain, which explained most of the rather dynamic and macho nicknames with which he'd been saddled by his peers. Standing next to his partner—who, with a name like Cane Canyon, might as well have been a fucking cowboy or an out of work porn star—Abell looked like the after photo in a before and after shot. As in, "This is what I looked like *after* I had dozens of rounds of radiation and chemotherapy and lost the will to live." He was called *Ack Ack* and *Double A* for the same reason that most of the guys at the office called Cane *Tiny*. It was their attempt at irony.

Nevertheless, despite his rather unimpressive appearance and pitifully out of date wardrobe, Abell was as tough as they came—gruff but pleasant, and informal but precise. Though he looked perpetually sleepy, he prided himself on his alertness and attention to detail. His appearance was disarming and completely belied the competence hidden within his small frame. Despite his appearance, and the fact that he was always thought to be a *nerd* or a *geek* (or a *Poindexter* as his daughters called him—both behind his back and to his face) by the same co-workers who had given him such ridiculous nicknames, he was built out of iron.

After a distinguished career as a combat engineer within the United States Air Force's 819th RED HORSE squadron, which had only come to an end as a result of multiple wounds he had suffered when his unit had come under small arms fire during a mission in Afghanistan, he had chosen to apply the many skills he had learned as a **R**apid **E**ngineer **D**eployable **H**eavy **O**perational **R**epair **S**quadron **E**ngineer to the private sector. After having made a king's ransom working first for Procter & Gamble and later for Total Quality Logistics, and after having seen the violence and horror of white supremacist terrorist attacks in Charleston, South Carolina, and in Charlottesville, Virginia, play out on his TV, his interests had changed. Using his prior military connections to land a job in the field of federal law enforcement, he had been employed by the FBI for the past five years. And for each of those five years, he had been partnered with Cane Canyon, who was already a fifteen-year-veteran with "The Bureau" when Abell first met him in 2018.

As he brushed his teeth and shaved, he turned on the last AM/FM clock radio known to man. It could only pick up one channel—unfortunately, a mindless AM news-talk-radio station—and it was preset to a volume just loud enough to carry over the sound of the shower. Ostensibly, this was so that he could catch the news while getting ready in the morning. In reality, however, he kept it just loud enough to wake up his wife each morning. If the inane observations of the neo-Fascist host of the morning drive program (whose "opinions" had last been culturally relevant sometime before the Vietnam War) didn't wake Felicity up, she might spend the entire day in bed; and if she did, who then would play tennis and golf with Carrie,

Samantha, Miranda, and Charlotte (or whatever his wife's friends' names were) all day?

As he entered the shower, the cultural relic on the radio finished telling a joke that he had broadcast over the air at least once a week for the better part of a millennium. And, when he got to the punchline ("Jesus Saves, but Moses invests"), the host laughed as if he was telling the joke for the very first time.

It must be nice to be the host of your own radio program, Abell thought to himself. Even if—like Gary, or Jerry, or Geoff, or whatever his name was— you were a pro-gun, anti-choice, sexist, racist, homophobic, xenophobic, Islamophobic, anti-Semitic, science-denying, flat-Earther who worshipped at the altar of the high priest of mumbo-jumbo, you still got to spend your time (and someone else's money) spewing your hatred and ignorance all over a captive audience that simply wanted to know whether or not the Reds had won last night and whether or not it was going to rain today. The amount of venom, to say nothing of the tragically bad jokes, that Abell had to wade through just to get to the top-of-the-hour news made him almost physically ill. But how else was he going to find out whether or not the Roebling Suspension Bridge was closed due to another fake bomb threat?

Maybe I should just break down and get a new radio, Abell thought to himself. *Then I could listen to something else . . . .* anything else *. . . . in the morning.*

But just as he considered entering the twentieth century by purchasing an electronic device made within the past fifty years, Abel heard his precious "better half" bitching about the volume from the bedroom. Sporting a smile that was pure sinister delight, he decided that the radio he had was just right.

Abell turned the radio down . . . ever so slightly, but the bitching continued. Perhaps it was the temperature in their bedroom today that was the problem. After all, he had bravely and brazenly set the thermostat at 73 degrees the night before, rather than at the customarily ordained 66 degrees. Abell's bold move, which had prevented him from feeling like he had awoken in *Ice Station Zebra,* had apparently rendered the master bedroom into "a blazing inferno."

Felicity's complaints were drowned out by the radio host's attempt at another joke—this one having to do with an asteroid which had recently changed jobs, hoping for something new, where it could "really make an impact."

Abell groaned once at the joke and groaned again when his twenty-year-old cell phone began to vibrate on the bathroom vanity; for as much as he looked forward to leaving for work every day, phone calls at 5:30 am on a Monday were like the unexpected arrivals of Generals in Iraq. They were "generally" (pun fully intended) not sources of good news.

Before he could even get out of the shower, Felicity noted the obvious, shouting "Abell, your fucking phone is ringing! Would you please answer it?"

His earlier smile had now vanished almost completely.

CHAPTER THREE

As Cane pulled into his reserved parking spot outside the FBI's Cincinnati field office (located in the rather affluent suburb of Kenwood), he noticed a red light on Laverne's dashboard indicating that her engine had begun to overheat . . . again.

That was not an unusual occurrence.

In fact, the stop and go traffic from Over the Rhine to Kenwood often caused the temperamental fifty-five-year-old engine to run excessively hot. The irony was that it took Cane several minutes to get the engine to warm up in the morning; but almost as soon as he had it ready to go, it quickly began to overheat. Which was precisely why he had named the car Laverne in the first place.

Laverne was a cougar Cane had met and bed in the summer of 2002, when he was in his early, and impressionable, twenties. Laverne, who had been just north of forty at the time, had been an eager and more than capable lover who, like the car which bore her name, took a while to . . . *warm up*. But, once she did—oh, Lord, how quickly she turned . . . and stayed . . . very hot! As his lurid thoughts turned back to one particularly delightful . . . *session* . . . he had spent with Laverne, he noticed that the radio was playing *The Mamas & the Papas* classic 1966 hit song "Monday, Monday."

Ironically, Cane could not remember ever having heard that song being played on the local classic rock station before, which was the only one Laverne's antiquated radio could seem to get on a semi-regular basis. And just as he turned off Laverne's engine, the song reached the point where Denny Doherty intoned:

> "Monday, Monday
> Can't trust that day
> Monday, Monday
> Sometimes it just turns out that way
> Oh, Monday mornin'
> You gave me no warnin'
> of what was to be . . ."

Great! If that's meant to be a fuckin' omen, God, I could do without the humor. It's not even 6:30, for Christ's sake, he mused inwardly. Failing to appreciate the irony of his having taken Jesus' name in vain while cursing the Lord, Cane got out of Laverne and, once again, played the voicemail message that he already listened to three times on his way in from home.

The message was from Jed Meadodo himself and simply said, "Good mornin,' pardner." For the life of him, Cane could not figure out why his boss affected some kind of exaggerated Matthew McConaughey drawl every time he spoke to him. Rolling his eyes, he continued to play the message: "I got a real interestin' varmint waitin' for you when you finally roll in here. So why don't you round up a posse and head on in to work? That is, unless you got somethin' better to do this mornin.' And let's try to be here before noon, okay, pardner?"

Cane winced, less at the absurd country twang, and more at the insinuation that he was prone to arriving late to work. In his entire career with "The Bureau," Cane had been late exactly once—and that had been a direct result of the aforementioned Laverne (the car, not the lover) having taken an unusually long time to warm up that morning. Every other day, he was in the office, at his desk, by no later than 7:00 am—which was usually a full two hours before his idiot boss strolled in.

As Cane deleted the obnoxious voicemail, he saw his partner, sadly entombed in that pathetic Dodge Caravan of his, ease into the parking lot. As he approached the "Beige Bitch," Cane just shook his head.

"How many miles do you have on that thing now, Abell?"

Abell greatly appreciated the fact that Cane never, not even once, referred to him by any one of his many different—all equally obnoxious—nicknames. However, he could certainly live without starting each workday with the same question. Unable to come up with anything better than the usual, Abell got out of the "Beige Bitch," took a sip from his third Diet-Coke of the morning and answered, "247,123 miles, Cane. 247,123. Which, I believe, is only slightly more than the cases of gonorrhea you've had since I bought the car, you sex crazed cowboy."

"Why don't you get rid of that thing and upgrade to something at least built this century?" Cane teased.

"What . . . like Laverne?"

"Hey—Laverne is a classic."

"Yeah . . . just like that classic piece of shit on your hip there." Abell was referring to Cane's Colt Cobra .38 special. While most agents, like Abell, now carried the standard-issue SIG Sauer P226 9mm pistol, Cane, for reasons passing understanding, insisted on sticking with his stainless steel, six shot revolver.

"Hey—it's a classic, too."

"A classic with a busted firing pin. Have you gotten that fixed yet?"

"I told you, it's not the firing pin," Cane answered. "It just has a temperamental transfer-bar. And it's still a classic."

Abell shook his head. "Yeah, a *classic* with a *temperamental transfer-bar* that's going to get you killed some day. Or, worse, get me killed. When was the last time you had that . . . *classic* . . . piece of shit out on the range?"

Quickly changing the subject, Cane held up his cellphone and said, "I don't know. But did you get a call from *Señor Fuck Face* this morning?"

Smiling back at Cane, Abell answered, "The only thing I find more bizarre than the fact that you call our boss—who has absolutely no Hispanic heritage whatsoever—*Señor Fuck Face* is the fact that, whenever he calls me, he sounds like he's doing a bad Billy Crystal impersonation. Why does he do that?"

Cane laughed. "Actually, I think he's going for a Mel Brooks thing, You know, like from *Blazing Saddles*?"

"But why? What about me reminds him of either Billy Crystal or Mel Brooks?"

"Ya really want me to answer that, pardner?" Cane responded, imitating the annoying twang his boss had used when he had left his message.

This time it was Abell's turn to laugh. "You got the Matthew McConaughey thing again?"

By way of confirmation, Cane answered, "Alright, alright, alright," in an even worse drawl than before. "Hook 'em horns, baby."

"Maybe he's going for a John Wayne thing, and he just doesn't know how to pull it off," Abell speculated.

"Are you kidding me? That assclown wouldn't know the difference between John Wayne and Fort Wayne."

"I suppose you're right. Why should voices be any different than anything else he does? He's always going off half-assed, half-cocked, and shit-brained."

Slipping neatly into their practiced routine of carrying on entire conversations by quoting dialogue from classic sitcoms, Cane smiled and answered by saying, "Yep, this time he took his gun and his toothbrush . . ."

"Shooting off his mouth again . . ." Abell responded instantly.

Quickly and seamlessly switching from *M*A*S*H* to *Seinfeld*, Cane finished their analysis of their "superior" by adding, "And he wants to be my Latex salesman?"

Doing an exaggerated spit take that involved a healthy dose of Diet-Coke coming out of his nose, Abell asked, "How do you always do that? Do you just sit around watching old reruns all day long, just trying to memorize the perfect line for the perfect situation?"

"Hey, when you're dealing with 247,123 cases of gonorrhea, you have a lot of free time on your hands."

Shaking his head in disbelief, Abell said, "That's not the only thing you have a lot of on your hands. How's . . . um, what's her name? The cocktail waitress/aspiring actress/spokesmodel you met last month? Glitter?"

"Giessel. Her name's Giessel. At least I think it was. Anyway, she's old news."

"You just met her last week!"

"And this is a whole *new* month, which makes her *old* news. I have since upgraded to Sasha."

"Unbelievable!" Abell said as the pair reached the front doors of the building.

"Speaking of old news, how's Felicity? Are you getting any?"

"No. I've been reduced to penguin sex."

"What's penguin sex?" Cane asked, playing along, although he already knew the answer.

"We just do it once a year now. And when we do, it's ice cold."

Shifting the conversation now into dialogue from *Friends*, Cane asked, "So . . . how long has it been since . . . you know? *Since you grabbed a spoon?*"

Without missing a beat, Abell responded, "Do the words *'Billy don't be a hero'* mean anything to you?"

"That bad, huh?"

"It's fine. At least I'm at work now. Let's go see what *Señor Fuck Face* is all hot and bothered about."

"There you go!" Cane said, patting his partner on the back as the two entered the building. Then, as the pair presented their credentials, without even realizing it, Cane begin to softly sing, *"But Monday mornin' couldn't guarantee that Monday evenin' you would still be here with me."*

CHAPTER FOUR

The FBI field office in Kenwood, Ohio, was a modern, four-story building lacking the musty odor, as well as any sense of the character, usually associated with a government building or a courthouse. While sterile and boring, it was clean, bright, and efficient—and in every other way, completely unremarkable.

Jed Meadodo's office was the only part of the building that was appointed luxuriously. Its soft lighting, thick wall-to-wall carpeting, leather chairs, and charming appointments which seemed to accompany any senior level executive—to say nothing of the infamous ego wall (which included diplomas, commendations, various awards and citations, and dozens of pictures of him gladhanding with a wide range of elected officials from "both sides of the aisle")—were all meant to exude a sense of calm and power, clearly indicating that this was the room where "the boss" worked.

Taller than Abell but shorter than Cane, Jed was so thin that he seemed almost rawboned. He was going prematurely bald and stared out at the world through an obscenely expensive pair of Tom Ford tortoiseshell glasses that he did not really need. He was always fastidious about his appearance and, at least for a civil servant, unusually well-dressed. Believing (although no one else did) that he bore a striking resemblance to a young Robert DeNiro, he was extremely sure of himself. However, there also emanated from him a well-practiced aloofness—an artifice which came from a lifetime of pretending to be whatever the person currently in front of him wanted him to be; and Abell, who possessed a legendary sixth sense (bordering on ESP) for determining whether or not someone was telling the truth, had long ago come to the conclusion that the moment Meadodo left a room, he became someone else. As a result, while his partner preferred bawdier sobriquets like *Señor Fuck Face*, Abell had always referred to their boss simply as "the mayor."

"Good morning, gentlemen," the director said as the two entered his office. Cane already knew from the smile on the little shit's face that it was going to be bad news. It seemed that there was nothing the smug bastard enjoyed more in life than the pleasure of dumping a lousy assignment on someone he didn't like. And Meadodo disliked Cane about as much as anyone in the office. Perhaps it was Cane's intimidating size; or, maybe it was his weathered good looks—flinty eyes and curly salt and pepper hair that combined to give him the look of a 1950s movie star—which were a source of envy, especially because they contrasted greatly with his own thin face, high cheekbones, and frog eyes which made him look perpetually surprised. But whatever it was, something about Cane rubbed Meadodo the wrong way, and he took great delight in dumping shitty assignments on the large man's shoulders. He even had the gall to bask in a glow of feigned magnanimity when he did the unloading.

"Director," was all Abell said by way of a response, while Cane said nothing at all.

"Have a seat, please," the director said, indicating the two Hancock and Moore leather chairs on the other side of his desk.

As Abell sat down comfortably, wondering if the furniture in the boss's office cost more than the combined tuitions of his three daughters, Cane poured himself with great difficulty into his own chair, seeming to positively expand into it until nothing more could be seen of it.

"I'm sorry to have bothered you both so early this morning," Jed lied, "but CPD sent a very unusual case our way over the weekend." He passed a thin manila file folder across the desk to Abell while Cane said, "CPD?"

"The Cincinnati Police Department," Meadodo pointed out unnecessarily.

"I know what it stands for, *director*. But why is CPD handing a case up to us? Please tell me it's not another money laundering case. You know we just wrapped up the Strunk case, and it was a real bitch."

"No, nothing quite that complicated, I'm sure. It appears that some lunatic walked right into their District Five precinct house and surrendered himself up. He then began confessing to having committed all sorts of crimes."

"What *sorts of crimes*?" Abell asked, opening the file.

Ignoring him, the director continued, "Well, I shouldn't say that he confessed to committing them. Rather, he confessed to being part of a vast conspiracy to commit a web of federal crimes. I was thinking it sounded very much like a RICO case."

The Racketeer Influenced and Corrupt Organizations (RICO) act was a federal law enacted by Congress in 1970 through Title IX of the Organized Crime Control Act. Signed into law by President Nixon, it provided for extending criminal penalties as well as civil causes of action for acts performed as part of an ongoing criminal investigation, and was designed primarily to go after organized crime. However, Director Meadodo, believing that everything was either mob related or a vast left-wing conspiracy to defraud the government, falsely assumed that virtually every case which came across his desk was a RICO case. In reality, they almost never were.

"What sorts of crimes?" Abell repeated. "What crimes did he confess to being a part of that fall under federal jurisdiction?"

Either because he didn't know or because he had grown bored with the conversation, Meadodo began to focus on something else on his calendar and simply said, "Oh, the usual. Presidential assassinations, treason, things like that. I'm sure it's all in the file."

As Cane began to wonder if he had missed a presidential assassination since the murder of John Kennedy sixty years earlier, he asked, "Have you read the file, *sir*?"

"Of course not, Agent Canyon. That's what I have you for." Then, apropos of nothing, he added, "How did a Polish American end up with a name like Cane Canyon, anyway?"

"*Siedzieć jak na tureckim kazaniu*," Cane mumbled by way of a response, glancing over to his partner as he said it. The literal translation to this Polish idiom was "sitting as if in a Turkish sermon." It was never made clear to

Cane by his father if there was a reason why it was the Turkish language that was used in this expression; in fact, he supposed that any language that was not widely spoken in Poland would have served just as well. In any event, the saying meant to suggest that the speaker was in a situation in which he had absolutely no clue as to what was happening around him, or what people were talking about.

"I beg your pardon," the director snapped testily.

"Don't mind him, Director," Abell advised. "He just has flies in his nose this morning." Abell, who was well acquainted with his partner's various idioms and expressions, had used another one of them to suggest that Cane was simply in a bad mood.

"*Mieć muchy w nosie,*" Cane mumbled, translating what Abell had said into Polish.

"Oh, yes, I see," Meadodo responded, as if he truly understood. "In any event, your "perp" is currently "cooling his heels" in one of the "sweatboxes" downstairs. I'd like you two to get down there right away to see what he has to say."

The fact that Meadodo, a career bureaucrat with about as much genuine law enforcement experience as Barney Fife, frequently used "cop talk" (particularly slang that was hopelessly out of place anywhere other than inside a Mickey Spillane novel) drove both Abell and Cane crazy. In fact, more than once, Cane had said that his boss's use of such out-of-date terms "made his balls itch."

In any event, the two dutifully took the file and proceeded to leave the director's office when Jed fired off one more parting shot. "And Officer Canyon, I'd still like to know how you came about such an unusual name. Perhaps we could *do lunch* together sometime this week to discuss it."

"*Wypchać się sianem,*" was all Cane offered by way of a response.

When the director looked to Abell for a translation, he simply shook his head and said, "Don't ask."

As the director's smile faded, the pair exited his office and approached the nearest stairwell. (For reasons he had never articulated to anyone, not even to his partner, Cane hated elevators and escalators and would not go anywhere near either of them.)

"*Do lunch*?" Cane asked. "What is he now? A fucking Hollywood executive producer or something?"

"Ah, forget about it. But *I* have a question for you."

"What?"

"How exactly did you come about that name?" Abell asked, just to further irritate his partner.

"I changed it when my parents passed away."

"Nah, what was it *before* you changed it?" Abell responded in a thick Scottish accent, knowing that "the routine" would restore his partner's earlier good mood.

"Giuseppe Petri," Cane responded, using his best Andy Garcia impersonation.

"Geez, I knew it! That's all you need, one thieving Pollock on the team!" Abell answered, altering ever so slightly Sean Connery's next line from *The Untouchables.*

Sufficiently cheered up now, Cane smiled and said, "Come on, let's go . . .

But Abell joined him so that they said in unison, ". . . to protect the property and the citizenry of . . ."

By the time they reached the next flight of stairs, both men were laughing.

It was the last laugh they would share for the next several hours.

CHAPTER FIVE

The "sweat box," as Jed Meadodo had so lovingly referred to one of the FBI's interrogation rooms, was no misnomer. These small rooms, which measured approximately eight feet in length and five feet in width, were no bigger than a three-room apartment's dining area. While they were soundproof, they also contained state-of-the-art audio and video equipment so that detectives in other parts of the office could see and hear everything.

As Abell and Cane entered the small room, made even smaller when Cane took up half of the available space and oxygen, they were somewhat surprised by what they saw. The man who was seated and handcuffed to the table in front of them was unremarkable in every way. From his build to his facial features, and from his boring clothes to his calm demeanor, he struck both agents as being precisely the sort of person who would forever be at the end of every line that ever formed in society. In short, he was the face in the faceless crowd, blending in until lost among the other faces. He seemed aloof, cold, and remote. Yet Abell perceived something oddly intimate about the jail-pallid and soft-eyed little man sitting on the other side of the interrogation table. And when their eyes first met, a brief sense of familiarity flashed between them. But it vanished as soon as he started to speak.

Even before Cane or Abell could ask him his name or whether or not he had been advised of his rights, he began saying in a low but distinct voice, "Good morning, officers. Or should I say agents? I'd introduce myself to you, but my name is irrelevant and, likely as not, neither of you would be able to pronounce it anyway. As my time is almost certainly extremely limited, I shall come directly to the point. I am from a planet as yet unknown to your people, and I come to you, as I did to the police officers who sent me here, with four pieces of urgent information. First, for slightly more than the past century, my people have been observing the activities of your people and, since 1947 on your calendar, have been actively interfering in your social, political, and economic affairs. Second, I know this because I have personally been an active part of this plot—a conspiracy to prevent your people from advancing beyond your primitive understanding of the universe. Third, I openly admit that my people and I have done immeasurable harm to your people, and I do not come to you now with a plan for making amends—for no . . . *penance* . . . as you might call it, is possible for me. I do, however, wish to leave this mortal coil you call Earth knowing that I have done my best to prevent what is next to come. Contrary to what many of your people think, there is an Intelligent Designer of the universe, something you might call God, and I fear that I would never get to meet that entity if I did not take this opportunity to atone, albeit in some small way, for the many crimes committed by my people. Finally, I have nothing to gain and everything to lose by disclosing this information to you; so you can rest assured that I am, albeit at great risk to my own well-being, telling you the truth."

The silence that reigned in the small room after their "perp" had finished his bizarre and shocking monologue was deafening. He sat there silently as Cane and Abell stared first at him and then at each other.

After the silence became painfully awkward, Abell closed up the manilla file folder his boss had given him and said, "Would you excuse us for just a minute. We'd like to go grab a cup of coffee. Can I get you anything? Coffee? A doughnut?"

"Or a straitjacket?" Cane added.

"No, thank you. I'm fine. I assume you'll need to speak to your superiors now. I'll wait here."

Abell just smiled back at the crazed lunatic as he and Cane stood and exited the room.

"Zrobili mnie w konia," Cane muttered, his latest idiom implying that someone had made a horse of him—the Polish version of someone having made an ass of him.

"I'll say," Abell agreed. "You think Jed's pulling an elaborate practical joke on us?"

"If it's a joke, it's both funny and well-executed. But I think you and I both know that it isn't."

"You think the boss's cheese has finally slid off his cracker?"

Cane sighed heavily.

"Only one way to find out. Let's go back up and see him."

*****

"This nutjob is cuckoo-for-Cocoa-Puffs," Cane assured his boss when they had been readmitted into his office. "Why isn't he at UC Medical Center . . . or Christ Hospital? Don't they both have outstanding psychiatric facilities?"

"Are you speaking from experience, Agent Canyon?" Meadodo asked.

"Listen, boss," Abell interjected, trying to calm the waters some. "This guy is clearly a mental case, or he's jacked up on seven different kinds of drugs. Either way, he doesn't belong here. Have you seen him or heard him? He thinks he's an alien for Christ's sake. Why don't we just send him back to CPD and let them deal with him?"

"Like Herod Antipas?"

"Excuse me?"

"Herod Antipas. He was the King of Judea who sent Jesus back to Pontius Pilate when . . ."

"I know who he was," Cane protested. "But what does he . . . ?"

While Meadodo pecked away at his cellphone, clearly indicating that he had better and more important things to do, he interrupted Cane by saying, "CPD administered a series of blood tests when your "perp" turned himself in on Friday afternoon. He's as clean as a whistle. He's not on anything—not even caffeine. In fact, he might well be the healthiest man alive. He also has no prior record; in fact, he doesn't seem to have much of a record of any kind. No Social Security number. No driver's license. No tax or voting records. No identifiable birthmarks, and his fingerprints don't show up anywhere in any database we have access to."

Meadodo shifted from typing on his cellphone to typing on his computer before he continued. "As far as his mental acuity, CPD brought in two specialists over the weekend and they examined him for hours. They even polygraphed the prick. He's sane, articulate, and is telling the truth—or at least he thinks he is enough to beat the machine."

"So what is he then, a spy or something?" Abell asked.

"Who gives a shit what he is. Interview him, see if there's anything we can hold him on while you attempt to verify his story, and then cut him loose."

Abell and Cane looked at each other.

"Attempt to verify his story? And how do you suggest we go about doing that?" Cane asked.

"I don't know. Go watch a few episodes of *Star Trek* with him and see if they corroborate his story."

"You're loving this, aren't you, sir?" Abell asked. "That's why you stuck Captain Crazy Pants with us, isn't it?"

"On the record, no. I'm just fulfilling my duty to make sure that any and all credible threats to the well-being and/or national security of this great nation are taken seriously and investigated to the fullest extent possible."

"And off the record?"

"Of the record, Agent Adamson. You bet your ass I'm enjoying it. Now, if you two will excuse me, I have not yet had my bran muffin this morning. Have fun with your . . . *person of interest*. I look forward to reading your full report on the matter. Good day, gentlemen."

As the director excused himself from his own office, Abell looked at Cane. "What, no great Polish or Russian expressions for this one?"

Cane just glared at his partner, a dark cloud passing over his face. Finally he said, *"Möge die Macht mit dir sein."*

Abell looked perplexed. "I don't think you've used that one before. What's that mean?"

"It's not Polish. It's German; it means 'May the Force be with you.' Let's go."

As Cane stood to leave, Abell laughed and responded, "Beam me up, Scotty."

PART TWO

Just Another Manic Monday

CHAPTER SIX

"You do need someone to 'beam you *up*,' you fucking midget," Cane said as the pair of agents made their way back downstairs to the sweat box. "How'd you end up so short anyway?"

"I don't know. How did you end up looking like George Clooney and Brock Lesnar had a Polish baby together?"

"Just lucky, I guess," Cane laughed.

But the laughter stopped when they reentered the interrogation room, with both men all business now.

"Okay, let's start over," Abell said. "I am agent Abell Adamson, and this ugly thing over here is my partner, Cane Canyon."

As the two agents resumed their seats, the man they were sent to question smiled and said, "I'm impressed."

"Why is that?" Cane wanted to know.

"Well, you just showed a remarkable level of intimacy and vulnerability by introducing yourself and your partner with your full names. I'm quite sure that your law enforcement protocols advise you no to do that."

"Yeah, we're all kinds of intimate and vulnerable," Cane quipped.

"Additionally," the man continued. "You are partners and have made it this far without killing each other."

The two agents just stared blankly at their "perp."

"Cain? Abel? The brothers from the Bible? The children of Adam and Eve? Why is it that humans never even bother to learn their own history?"

"I'm not sure that Adam and Eve constitute history," Abell replied.

"And they're not spelled the same," Cane added.

"Nevertheless, whether they are history or mythology, they are your stories. A society should always be well-versed with its own fables. We certainly are where I come from."

"Right . . . about that . . ." Cane started.

"That's the third reason I'm impressed. You two made it much farther than the police officers I met Friday night. Unlike them, you two made it all the way to the end of my speech before you left. Well done."

"Speaking of your speech . . ." Abell said, looking again at the contents of the file folder his boss had given him.

"All of it was true," the man assured him. "I am not what you would call a nice person, but I can't do anything about the harm I've already caused or the people I've already hurt. But I can at least try to do something about making sure no one else gets hurt."

"Okay, before we get into all of that, let's start with something easy," Cane suggested. "Let's start with your name."

"I told you before, you couldn't possibly pronounce it. Your tongues aren't hinged correctly to be able to speak my language. But, for simplicity's sake, please just call me Gabriel."

"*Gabriel?*" Abell asked. "Like the archangel from the Bible. God's herald?"

"Ah, top marks!" Gabriel said, elated. "So, you do know your own histories. Yes, the story of Gabriel held that he was sent by God to interpret a vision to Daniel and that he appeared to Mary in the account of the Annunciation in fables of Luke. In fact, he appears to have artificially inseminated Mary, thus accounting for her virgin pregnancy. He is also described in the Christian Bible as the guardian angel of Israel, defending its people against the angels of other nations."

"The *Gospel* of Luke," Cane corrected. "Not the *book* of Luke. And the . . . *stories* . . . of Gabriel are not fables. And nobody artificially inseminated anyone, okay?" Cane was a lapsed Catholic who, despite having several reservations about Catholic doctrine, didn't care to hear those reservations being espoused by someone he had just met—especially not someone who, for all intents and purposes, appeared to be a certifiable lunatic.

"I meant no offense," Gabriel assured Cane. "I was simply making the point that, like Gabriel, I bring important news. And I am the closest thing your planet has to a defender against . . . *the angels of other nations.*"

"Meaning aliens, right? Extraterrestrials? That's what you're trying to tell us?" Abell asked.

"Precisely!"

Cane rubbed his eyes while Abell sat back in his chair silently. After two minutes of awkward silence, Gabriel decided to break the tension. "Why do you find what I have to tell you so hard to believe?"

"Well, first of all, you haven't exactly told us anything yet," Cane pointed out.

"And, second, there isn't exactly a precedent for . . . whatever it is you're trying to do."

"Of course there is," Gabriel replied. "Starting with John of Patmos and his book of Revelation, there have been ample prophets and seers throughout human history."

"Name one," Cane challenged.

"I just did—John of Patmos."

"Name another."

"Cassandra, the Trojan priestess from Greek mythology who was dedicated to the god Apollo. Or the sixteenth-century French astrologer Nostradamus. Then there's the twentieth-century American psychic Charles Criswell King."

"*The Amazing Criswell?*" an incredulous Cane asked. "Isn't he the nut job who claimed that Denver, Colorado, would be struck by a ray from space that would cause all metal to adopt the qualities of rubber?"

"He also predicted that mass cannibalism and the end of the Earth would happen in August of 1999," Abell added. "I'd say he missed that one."

"Yes, and in March of 1963, he also predicted that your President Kennedy would not run for re-election in 1964 because something was going to happen to him in November of 1963. I would say he *nailed* that one." The last part of Gabriel's statement was made with a strikingly accurate impersonation of Abell's voice.

"Who else you got?" Cane asked.

"I beg your pardon?"

"Who. Else. You. Got? You got any other prophets who aren't dead or looney-tunes or both?"

"Madame Marie Anne Adelaide Lenormand."

"Who?" Abell asked.

"Also known as Marie Anne Le Normand, she was a French necromancer and fortune-teller of considerable fame during Napoleon's time."

Cane leaned in close to his partner. "Too bad she didn't have the foresight to warn old Napoleon not to invade Russia during the winter."

As Abell chuckled, Gabriel said, "Joan Ceciel Quigley. She was an astrologer who gave advice to the Reagans in the 1980s. In fact, she was called upon by First Lady Nancy Reagan in 1981 after John Hinckley tried to assassinate her husband, but we'll come to that later. There's also Giorgio Tsoukalos, the Swiss writer and television producer who was the first to correctly postulate that ancient alien astronauts interacted with ancient humans. And Filip Coppens, the Belgian writer and radio host who . . ."

Cane held up his hands in a display of mock surrender. "Okay, E.T. You win. Enough with the crystals, Tarot cards, and Ouija boards here." He sighed heavily before continuing. "Do you mind if I take a moment to feed the cancer genes, *Kreskin*?" he asked snidely as he stood up and reached for his lighter and pack of cigarettes.

Gabriel said nothing as Cane left the room, but once he was gone—ostensibly on his way outside, where he could enjoy his smoke in silence—Gabriel said, "Your partner doesn't seem to like me very much."

Closing the file and standing up, Abell said, "It's nothing personal. He's just in a bad mood because the Reds blew a 4-0 lead in the ninth inning last night."

Gabriel just stared blankly back at Abell.

"The Reds? Baseball? No? I guess they don't have that on planet Xanadu or Ork or wherever it is that you're from."

"Actually, the name of my planet is *Ev jiǎllar-θŭ*."

"Fine, *Ev jiǎllar-θŭ*. Please excuse me for a minute while I go and consult with my Biblical brother. We'll be back in a minute. In the meantime, do you need anything?"

"No," said an astonished Gabriel. "It is you who needs something."

"What do I need?"

"Time. And you're rapidly running out of it."

CHAPTER SEVEN

"Okay, Gabriel," Cane said when they began again. "Let's start with a little thing we agents like to call evidence. What *evidence*, if any, exists to prove that aliens are real . . . AND . . . that they have been involved in the formation of Earth's policies for the past century or so?"

"Your sarcasm notwithstanding, the evidence is overwhelming. How about the development of integrated-circuit technology? Or the super tenacity fibers that make Kevlar possible? GPS? LASERs? Microwaves? Night vision? Do you really think any of these could possibly have been invented by a people so primitive that it took you three days to figure out how to get bottled water to the Superdome after Hurricane Katrina? Could a society that still hasn't figured out how to get lead out of the water in Flint, Michigan, have possibly created stealth technology, depleted uranium shells, or fiber optics without some help? And could a nation like yours, whose commander-in-chief believes that stealth technology *literally* makes a plane invisible—like Wonder Woman's invisible jet—have developed smart bombs, silicon chips, and MASERs?"

"He has a point there," Cane muttered under his breath.

"And . . . *your people* . . . have helped us with all of that?" Abell asked, ignoring his partner as best he could.

"Of course not!" Gabriel chided. "In fact, we've done almost everything in our power to sabotage the advancement of your technology. However, as primitive as you remain, your progress has been aided immeasurably by ours—so much so that you now represent an existential threat to our very survival."

"But you just said that . . . and I can't believe I'm really saying this . . . that aliens haven't been helping us," Cane pointed out.

"Not willingly, no. But all of those advancements I just mentioned, to say nothing of things like "smart phones," which contain greater computing power than the Apollo 11 spacecraft that landed on the moon in 1969, were all made possible by reverse engineering the spacecraft that crashed in Roswell, New Mexico, in July of 1947."

"Roswell? *Right* . . ." Cane groaned as if he had just heard the world's worst Dad-joke.

"Do you not find it a coincidence that our vehicle was lost just two years after your Trinity Test? And just one hundred and seventeen miles away from the test site? I can assure you, that was no coincidence. While we had been monitoring you for approximately fifty years, you didn't become a real threat to us until you split the atom in the New Mexico desert in the summer of 1945, and then decided to weaponize that achievement. Then, after we saw you were barbaric enough to actually employ that weapon on your fellow man . . . well, let's just say we took a greater interest in you."

Rolling his eyes, Abell asked, "And the crash in New Mexico? What was that? Pilot error? Just ran out of gas? Flat tire?"

Cane chuckled while Gabriel shook his head. "No. Although your country did not successfully test detonate a hydrogen bomb until 1952—just five years *after* the Roswell crash, by the way—it continued to experiment with bigger and better atomic and thermonuclear weapons throughout the 1940s and early 1950s. In fact, we believe it was some form of a cobalt or neutron bomb your people were playing around with which knocked our spacecraft from the sky that night."

"You're saying that we nuked one of your UFOs, and that your people lived to tell about it?" Cane asked.

"In a sense, yes. The device you detonated . . . whatever it was . . . triggered some sort of an EMP burst which damaged our craft's navigational and operational systems. In short, you benefitted from your own incompetence."

"You're saying we got lucky?" Abell asked.

"You got lucky," Gabriel confirmed with a nod of his head.

After thirty seconds of silence, Cane asked, "What is an EMP burst? Is that like a UFO's photon torpedoes, or something?"

Before Gabriel could answer, Abell said, "It's short for electromagnetic pulse, cowboy. It's an intense burst of electromagnetic energy due to a sudden acceleration of charged particles. The resulting energy destroys any electronic device it comes across, and the effects could be spread to power lines, hospitals, automobiles, banks, supermarkets."

"Quite right," Gabriel agreed. "And it's potentially far more deadly than any kind of atomic or nuclear bomb."

Cane stared at his partner in awe while Garbiel just smiled.

"What?" Abell asked. "Didn't you ever see *War of the Worlds*?"

"What your partner failed to explain is that an EMP burst can also be a naturally occurring, transient, electromagnetic disturbance, and it can be caused by a variety of sources—including your own sun."

"*Our* own sun?"

"Yes. *We* have one of our own," Gabriel answered. "Two actually."

"Of course you do," Abell responded.

"And the solar flares cast by your sun are a near constant source of electromagnetic energy. That's why, during solar storms, cell phone and TV reception can be negatively affected."

"Let me go back a second," Cane said. "You said an EMP burst is potentially far deadlier than any kind of atomic or nuclear bomb."

"Yes. What of it?"

"Aren't they the same thing?"

Gabriel shook his head and practically tsk-tsked Cane. "No. *Atomic* bombs, like those your country dropped on Japan in 1945, rely on fission reactions—splitting the atom, as it were. *Nuclear* bombs, specifically hydrogen bombs, use an infinitely more complicated process of nuclear fusion rather than fission and, as a result, are much more powerful, and they release exponentially more energy than atomic bombs."

Seeing that his partner, as smart as he was, was hopelessly lost, Abell leaned over and said to him, "Think of it this way. When you and Glitter . . ."

". . . Giessel . . ." Cane corrected.

"Whatever. When you two first . . . *got together* . . . you generated a lot more heat, energy, and intensity than when you split up. Get it?"

"Then why didn't Doctor Spock over here just say it like that?" Cane wanted to know.

"*Mister* Spock," Abell corrected. "*Doctor* Spock was an egghead child psychoanalyst."

Now it was Gabriel's turn to roll his eyes and shake his head. "Explaining the basics of atomic energy by using human coitus as an example. It's amazing you people ever emerged from your caves."

"What? You don't like . . . what did you call it?.....*coitus*? You don't do that on your planet?"

"No! Of course not. Copulation is a rather messy, awkward, and utterly inefficient way of ensuring the continuation of the species."

"*You* don't have sex, and *we're* the primitive ones?! How advanced could a society be that doesn't like fucking?" Cane wanted to know.

"Then how do your people procreate?" Abell began.

"I'd explain the process to you, but I'm afraid it would upset both of you immeasurably. This is a very small room, and it would be made to feel even smaller if either, or both, of you vomited in here."

Cane exhaled loudly. "Okay . . . let's go back to something you said earlier. You said that your people . . . Jesus, Mary, and Joseph, I must be losing my mind . . . had been monitoring us for around fifty years *before* we test-detonated a nuclear . . . I'm sorry . . . an *atomic* bomb, right?"

"That's correct. Our interest in you didn't really begin until you started to experiment with flight."

"The Wright Brothers? In Kitty Hawk, North Carolina?" Abell asked; but before Gabriel could respond, Abell turned to his partner and said, "Did you know that my paternal grandfather, Joseph, worked in their bicycle shop in Dayton?"

"No shit?"

"No shit."

"That's wonderful," Gabriel complimented. "But I was referring to the *first* man-made flight, the one made by a man named John J. Montgomery in 1883. He flew his craft for a distance of approximately six hundred feet near San Diego, California—a full twenty years *before* the Wright Brothers."

Abell made a notation in the file he had on Gabriel.

"John J. Montgomery, huh? Never heard of him," Cane said.

"Nevertheless, once your people started experimenting with man-made flight apparatuses, it was only a matter of time before you started looking towards the stars. At the time, we had no idea that it would be only seventy-four more years before you started to place objects into a low Earth orbit. Nothing in your prior history indicated to us that you would be able to make that kind of a leap in such a brief time."

"Yeah, we're just full of surprises, aren't we?" Abell said, making another note in his file.

"Quite. After that first flight, we waited another thirty years or so to see what you would do next. Finally, by April of 1912, we could no longer ignore the obvious."

"Which was?" Cane asked.

"That your technology was advancing much faster than we thought was possible. So that's when we began to . . . *interfere*."

"Wait a minute," Abell said. "April of 1912? That's when the *Titanic* sank."

"Yes, it is. And now you know who was responsible for that."

CHAPTER EIGHT

"The *Titanic*?" said Cane, flabbergasted. "First of all, what does the *Titanic* have to do with man-made flight? And, second, everybody in the whole fuckin' world knows that it hit an iceberg and sank. Christ—they even made a movie about it."

"*Movies*—plural," Abell corrected. "I think there's like twenty of them now."

"Right! And in all of those movies, I never saw a single little green man. So what kind of shit are you trying to pull here, *Gabriel*? You may not believe this, but we have some *actual* investigative work to do." Cane then sat back in his chair and crossed his arms as if challenging Gabriel to prove him wrong.

In response, Gabriel smiled. "To address your first question, Agent Canyon, it's not just a question of man-made flight. To us, the bigger picture was the progress of human technological advances, and the *Titanic* was a big part of that. Second, despite the history you "learned" from Mister DiCaprio and Miss Winslet, that ship—which was cutting edge technology at the time—should have been able to simply shrug off a glancing blow from an iceberg—any iceberg. Even a mediocre student of physics can do the computation. Simply factor in the size of the *Titanic*, the speed at which she was moving, the thickness of her hull, and the angle at which she struck the iceberg, and you will find that the vessel would have done far more damage to the iceberg than to her own hull . . . unless that hull had been compromised first."

"That's bullshit," Cane surmised.

Massaging his chin in thought, Abell said, "I'm not so sure, cowboy. It's the same principle as the Twin Towers. If not for the ten thousand gallons of gasoline that exploded inside each building, the structures would have remained standing. They were built to shrug off a direct hit from a hurricane. They fell because the intense fire *inside* weakened the building trusses, not the blunt force trauma of the hits *outside*."

"And the same is true of the RMS *Titanic*," Gabriel assured him. "There was a fire on board the ship that was smoldering in coal bunker number six for approximately ten days *before* the ship left Belfast. That fire heated the hull bulkheads up to somewhere around 1,000 degrees Celsius, weakening the structural integrity of the hull by 75%. That's 1,832 degrees Fahrenheit, which is approximately the same temperature that was reached inside the impact zones in the two World Trade Center towers. And just as the weakened structural steel of those towers contributed to their collapse, so, too, did the weakened section of the *Titanic's* hull make it impossible for her to withstand the impact of the iceberg."

Total silence reigned in the "sweat box" for nearly two minutes.

Finally Abell spoke up. "There's one major problem with your theory, Gabriel."

"One?!" Cane shouted.

"Even if everything you just said is true, how could your people guarantee that the ship would strike the iceberg at precisely the spot where the fire had weakened the hull?"

Gabriel smiled at Abell before responding. "Well done, Agent Adamson. But you're assuming that it was our intent to have the ship strike an iceberg. It wasn't. That was just . . . good luck. Our hope had been that the fire, which we started, would be sufficient to sink the vessel."

"Good luck?" Cane challenged. "Fifteen hundred lives lost was *good luck?*"

When Gabriel didn't respond, Abell asked, "What useful purpose would have been served by sinking that ship?"

"If the *Titanic* went down . . . the ship that God himself wasn't supposed to be able to sink . . . and if it went down on its maiden voyage no less, which it did . . . well, just think of the setback that it would—and did— have on the psyche of the entire planet. It was a significant blow to human technological advancement for decades. At least that's what we had hoped. As it turns out, your people recovered and responded so quickly that we had to strike again—much sooner than what we had planned."

Silence reigned again, this time for only thirty seconds.

"You struck again?" Abell asked.

Cane turned to his partner and said, "Hold the phone there, *Ack Ack*. You're not starting to believe this shit are you?"

Stunned by his partner's first-ever use of one of his nicknames, Abell just stared curiously at Cane. After what he felt was an appropriately long time, he turned back to Gabriel and repeated himself. "You struck again?"

"Yes. I'm afraid so," Gabriel confirmed.

"Where? When?" Cane challenged.

"Lakehurst, New Jersey. May 6, 1937."

*****

The two agents excused themselves and, once again, left the interrogation room so that they could stand outside, where Gabriel could not hear them.

"You know where he's going next, right?" Cane asked. "Lakehurst, New Jersey? 1937? He's talking about the *Hindenburg*, Abell."

"I know."

"So what's he going to tell us? That little green men blew it up after they sank the *Titanic*? Then what? That aliens bombed Pearl Harbor?"

"I get it. He's crazier than an outhouse rat."

"So what are we supposed to do with him?"

Abell paused for just a moment before answering. "I'm sure there's a room with padded walls somewhere that has space for him."

"I don't think it's as simple as that anymore."

"What do you mean?"

Cane paced in circles for a minute before responding. "Okay, he's batshit crazy, right? We agree upon that. But it's not like he's sitting in there drooling and rubbing his own shit all over the place."

"What are you saying?" Abell asked.

"I'm saying that he doesn't present himself like your run-on-the-mill Looney Tunes nutcase. He's totally lucid, and he comes across as poised, articulate, educated . . . even urbane."

"Whoa there, cowboy? Are you telling me that you're starting to believe his . . . stories from beyond? He's a walking/talking *Twilight Zone* episode."

"Agreed," said Cane. "I don't believe a word he's saying. But the way he's saying it . . . well, it's a little alarming. The guy might not be a harmless nutcase. He actually believes everything he's saying. You can see it in his expression."

"But he's lying," Abell pointed out. "Or he's delusional."

"That's precisely my point. He's either a pathological liar or he's schizophrenic. But I'm afraid there might be more to it than that. He might also be a psychopath . . . or a sociopath."

"Is there a difference between the two?" Abell asked.

"Hell if I know. Before I met E.T. in there, I thought atomic bombs were the same thing as nuclear weapons, so what do I know about anything?"

Abell went to the nearest vending machine to procure another Diet-Coke, his fourth of the day, and took a long sip before saying anything more. "Then I guess we just go back in there and keep him talking. If he's harmless, we'll have a hell of a story to tell at the next Bureau picnic."

"And if he isn't harmless?" Cane asked, desperate for another cigarette.

"Then maybe he'll slip up and confess to the Kennedy assassination. Who knows? Maybe he knows where Jimmy Hoffa is buried. We could become famous after all of this."

Cane didn't smile at his partner's joke. Instead he said, "I need another cigarette before we go back in there."

"Go ahead. I need to see a guy about a horse anyway."

"You wouldn't have to piss so much if you didn't drink twelve of those every day," Cane pointed out as Abell finished off his drink.

Pointing at the cigarette that Cane had already taken out, Abell responded. "And you'd live a lot longer if you'd just shove those up your ass instead of smoking them."

Looking at his cigarette oddly, Cane said. "Hmmmm. Never thought of that. Sasha is into that sort of stuff. Maybe . . ."

"I beg you not to finish that sentence, cowboy. Go have your cigarette and I'll meet you back here. Then we can find out how Luke Skywalker in there crashed the *Hindenburg*."

CHAPTER NINE

"So, tell us all about the *Hindenburg* disaster, Gabriel," Cane said when he and his partner reentered the sweat box. "Are you going to tell me now that, in addition to sinking the actual *Titanic*, you also arranged for a bolt of lightning to strike the "*Titanic* of the sky," igniting the helium inside?"

Gabriel chuckled and looked at both agents. "Did you just get that off of Google? Or are you testing me?"

Neither agent said anything.

Waiting for an appropriate amount of time, Gabriel finally started to explain. "The *Hindenburg* was not struck by lightning. Nor was it inflated with helium. It was levitated by sixteen gigantic cotton bags filled with hydrogen. Hydrogen is lighter than helium and provides greater lifting power. In fact, hydrogen is the lightest element on your Periodic Table of Elements. There are much lighter gases than that, but you are not yet aware of them."

"Isn't hydrogen much more flammable than helium?" Cane asked, reciting something that he had, in fact, just looked up on the internet.

"Yes. But in addition to hydrogen being lighter than helium, it was also more readily available to the Germans in 1937. In the 1930s, the only country on your planet that produced helium was the United States, and the US was not "in business" with the Nazis—at least not for chemicals, anyway. Politically, elements of your government were very much "in bed" with the Nazis, but that's not really relevant to our discussion."

Cane and Abell just looked at each, not even bothering to roll their eyes anymore.

"So tell us . . . how did you do it?" Cane asked.

"Quite simply, as a matter of fact. Steel wires surrounded all sixteen of the inflated gas bags, securing them in place. We managed to damage several of them before the zeppelin ever left Germany. With those wires unsecured, all that was needed was to create a leak of the hydrogen. This was done by having someone aboard the vessel fire a couple of shots into two of the gas bags. Those shots ruptured bags four and five, allowing hydrogen to escape. Once oxygen mixed with the released hydrogen, LZ129 . . . the *Hindenburg* . . . was turned into a gigantic floating bomb."

"But the investigators ruled out sabotage," Abell pointed out, skeptical.

"Yes, but only after they had named two suspects, searched the wreckage and found the firearm that we had used, and discovered a set of very suspicious tire tracks leading away from the crash site. Those same investigators who *ruled out sabotage* were very close to the actual truth."

"Go on," Abell said.

"At 7:25 pm, a spark coming either from charged particles releasing static electricity or from one of the loose metal cables inside the dirigible ignited the now combustible gases leaking from the aft fuel cells. The mix of oxygen and hydrogen in the air acted as fuel, and the flames quickly spread, tracing the hydrogen back to its source and causing the fuel cells to explode. And the rest, as you say, is history."

"Why the *Hindenburg*? And why then? Hadn't it flown multiple times already?" Cane asked, already knowing the answer.

"Very good, Agent Canyon. You must have seen a movie about it. Yes, just the year before, it had made ten round trips between Germany and the US. This last fateful flight was the first one scheduled for 1937. We had tried something like this before. You're probably much less familiar with the R101 disaster."

Gabriel received confirmation of that assessment when the two agents stared back at him with bovine looks of curiosity.

"R101," Gabriel continued, was one of a pair of British rigid-airships completed in 1929 as part of Britain's Imperial Airship program. When it was built, it was the world's largest flying craft, 223 meters . . . I'm sorry, 731 feet . . . in length. In fact, it was not surpassed by another hydrogen-filled airship until LZ129, the *Hindenburg,* was launched seven years later. In October of 1930, using the same strategy we would later employ with the *Hindenburg,* we arranged for R101 to crash in France, during its maiden overseas voyage, killing forty-eight of the fifty-four people on board. While that crash effectively ended British airship development, it didn't achieve the desired effect of preventing other countries from stepping in to fill the void. In fact, even after the *USS Akron* was destroyed during a thunderstorm off the coast of New Jersey in 1933, killing seventy-three of the seventy-six crewmen and passengers . . . that one wasn't us, by the way; sometimes accidents really do happen . . . progress continued."

"So, why the *Hindenburg?*" the two agents asked almost simultaneously.

"Because, as you said, it was the *Titanic of the sky.* It was a flying five-star hotel, the pride of the Nazi air fleet. At over 245 meters . . ."

"Around 804 feet," Abell said to Cane.

". . . it was the largest aircraft ever to fly. So confident and arrogant were its designers and operators that they actually allowed the passengers on board to smoke. Can you imagine that? Anyway, as your people are now wont to say, *If it didn't happen on CNN, it didn't happen.* So we arranged for it to happen in Lakehurst, New Jersey—just seventy-five miles from New York City, the capital of the world. It was there that a worldwide radio audience would be able to hear Herbert Morrison's memorable broadcast of the crash."

"Oh, the humanity," Cane mimicked.

Gabriel nodded. "Precisely. That crash effectively ended all human commercial and passenger airship flights. However, what we did not anticipate was that those flights would have soon ended anyway. The advent of airplanes made air travel much faster and more efficient, and at a fraction of the cost."

"So, then what?" Abell asked.

"I'm sorry."

"Then what? After your people allegedly sank the *Titanic* and blew up the *Hindenburg*, then what? It seems like man's technological progress didn't exactly slow down as a result of those two setbacks."

"You're quite right," Gabriel agreed. "But then we realized that your continued advancement was something of a blessing. So we stopped trying to inhibit it—at least momentarily."

"What do you mean by *a blessing*," Cane wanted to know.

Gabriel shifted uncomfortably in his chair and took a deep breath. "By the late 1930s, we came to understand that most of your technological development was being employed in the field of warfare. So, rather than continuing to try to inhibit it, we sought to leave it unchecked. By 1939, Japan was already at war all over the Pacific, and Germany and the Soviet Union had invaded Poland. The entire world was at war—again. For the second time in less than twenty-five years, man's technological "know how" was being directed towards bigger and better means of killing himself. Think of it: tanks, machine guns, barbed wire, land mines, submarines, airplanes, poison gas, flame throwers, napalm, radar. Considering the rate at which your technology was increasing, and the eagerness with which you were using those improvements to exterminate each other, the best thing we could do to ensure our own safety from you was to simply sit back and let you do it: exterminate yourselves, that is. Do you realize that there still aren't as many Jews alive in the world today as there were when Adolf Hitler came to power in 1933? Just think about that for a second. Then add to that holocaust the fire bombings of places like Dresden and Tokyo, the rape of Nanking, the Katyn Forest massacre. You were so busy creating a threat to your very own survival that we no longer viewed you as a threat to ours. Our fear that you might one day advance to the point where you could journey into the stars and come find us simply no longer existed."

"Until . . . ?" Abell asked.

"Until 5:29 am, Mountain War Time, on July 16, 1945."

"What happened then?" Cane asked.

"Then, in the ironically named *Jornada del Muerto* desert, about fifty-six kilometers . . . 35 miles . . . southeast of Socorro, New Mexico, on what was then the Alamogordo Bombing and Gunnery range, the leading scientists in the world . . . *became Death, the destroyer of worlds.*"

CHAPTER TEN

"You're talking about the Trinity test. The culmination of the Manhattan Project," Abell noted.

"Yes, I am. When he witnessed the detonation of that first atomic bomb, the father of that device, J. Robert Oppenheimer, quoted from the Bhagavad Gita and said, 'Now I am become Death, the destroyer of worlds'."

"Yeah, I just saw that movie. *Oppenheimer*? It came out the same weekend as *Barbie*, didn't it?" Cane asked.

Gabriel stared back at Cane with the same curious look a dog might give to a sound he'd never heard before.

"What is the Bhagavad Gita?" Abell asked.

"It is a Hindu scripture, written in Sanskrit. All seven hundred of its verses center on a dialog between a great warrior prince named Arjuna and his charioteer guide, Krishna, an avatar . . . or . . . incarnation . . . of Vishnu, the Hindu deity who created the universe."

"Great, but what's it got to do with the atomic bomb?" Cane asked.

"Does any of your knowledge of history come from anywhere other than movies?" Gabriel asked. But before Cane could answer, Gabriel explained: "As you no doubt saw in the film, when the bomb was successfully test-detonated, some who witnessed it laughed, a few others cried, but most of them were silent. But Oppenheimer, knowing that the world could not ever be the same, watched the fireball and turned to Hinduism to make sense of it all. While he was not a Hindu himself, Oppenheimer had always found that philosophy . . . religion . . . whatever we choose to call it . . . very useful in trying to understand the world, trying to give it some kind of meaningful structure. In Hinduism, the great god Vishnu is involved not only in the creation of the world, but also in its destruction. In chapter ten of the Bhagavad Gita, I forget which verse, Krishna says something to the effect that, irrespective of what Arjuna does or does not do, everything is in the hands of the divine."

"So you're saying that Oppenheimer thought he had become God in that moment . . . that he was divine?" Abell asked.

"Some God," Cane added, derisively. "A God who both creates and then destroys the world."

Looking perturbed, Gabriel answered Cane first. "And how is that any different from your Christian God? Did he not create the world and then destroy it all with a flood?" Before Cane could respond, Gabriel turned to Abell. "And no, I do not mean to imply that Oppenheimer felt, in that moment, that he had somehow become a god. However, in one of the verses of the Bhagavad Gita, Arjuna asks Krishna to reveal his universal form. And when Krishna obliges, he manifests as a sublime and terrifying being of many mouths and eyes. As Oppenheimer stared at that fireball he had created, he must have thought of Krishna. In fact, he later said, 'If the radiance of a thousand suns were to burst at once into the sky, that would be like the splendor of the mighty one.' Was he referring to the atomic bomb or to Vishnu—or both?"

"Does it matter?" Abell asked.

"No, I suppose it doesn't. Perhaps not to you. But it mattered very much to the hundreds of thousands who died in Hiroshima and Nagasaki. And it mattered a great deal to us."

"Why?" Cane asked.

"Because not only had you created a weapon capable of eliminating all life on your own planet, you now had the ability to eliminate all life on ours as well. And it was only a matter of time before you began to deploy that weapon into the heavens."

"So you were actually scared of us?" Cane asked quite smugly.

"Yes, quite so. Does that give you some sense of pride or satisfaction, Agent Canyon? Does it make you feel somehow taller or safer to know that you made my people feel smaller and less safe?"

"It don't exactly make me feel bad, if that's what you're asking."

Gabriel shook his head in disbelief. "Are you familiar with *Operation Paperclip*?" he asked.

"Can't say that I am, no," Cane lied. "You going to tell me now that we couldn't even invent the paperclip without the help of Martians and Wookies and Vulcans and God-only-knows who else?"

"*Operation Paperclip*," Gabriel said, unable to mask his annoyance, "was a secret United States intelligence program through which more than 1,600 German scientists, engineers, technicians, and mathematicians—many of whom, by the way, were former or even current leaders of the Nazi party—were spirited out of Germany, brought quietly to your country, and employed by your CIA, NSA, ONI, and other like-minded intelligence and counterintelligence agencies. Which means that your country, long before WWII was even complete, was already bringing some of the very people who you were still at war with—people who were responsible for the deaths of tens of millions—here to work on building the atomic bomb, instead of being prosecuted as war criminals. And why? Because you were more afraid of your ally, the Soviet Union, than you were of your two enemies, Germany and Japan. And it is for that reason that you allied so quickly with Germany and Japan, your recent enemies, after the war to wage a cold war against the Soviet Union, the ally that was indispensable to you in winning WWII."

"What's your point?" Cane asked, his temper starting to flare.

"I have many points. The two I choose to make right now are these. First, yes, my people were scared of your people. If you were capable of so easily changing enemies from one country to another, how difficult would it be for you to decide that my people were your new old enemy, just as you had done with the Soviets?"

"According to you, your people already were our enemy!" Cane reminded Gabriel, his voice raising to match his ire.

"What's your second point?" Abell asked calmly.

Taking a moment to let the tension ease and to allow Cane's outburst, which he had so carefully orchestrated, to subside, Gabriel smiled at the two agents and said, "My second point, as you just so capably demonstrated, Agent Canyon, is that . . . you are clearly starting to believe me."

Cane wanted to grab Gabriel by the throat and throttle him. Instead, he simply glared at him, eventually directing his attention towards his partner, prepared to ask him to step outside again. But something about his partner suddenly bothered Cane, something eerie and disturbing that he couldn't quite put his finger on. Abell was staring rather oddly at Gabriel and smiling with an expression that Cane couldn't quite place.

I may be wrong, he thought to himself, *but it seems to me like he is looking at that nutjob with a sense of . . . pride.*

For his part, Abell began to doubt his senses. Usually, he had a strong and accurate intuition about people. He could normally discern much about a person within just minutes of meeting him (or her), and he rarely wavered from that initial impression. But in Gabriel's case, he began to wonder if he had misread this man. *Perhaps, just perhaps, there is much more to this . . .*

But Gabriel cut off his musings. "Over the past seventy-eight years, ever since that fateful day in the New Mexico desert, my people have fully integrated ourselves into your society—such as it is. We have developed vast networks of influence in your governments, industries, and mass media, and we have done so to protect our own vital interests. Increasingly, however, the vital interests of your people have come into conflict with the vital interests of mine. And we are fast approaching a point of intersection. Soon . . . very soon, my people will no longer be content to simply meddle in your affairs. We will take . . . more active and aggressive measures. So it is good that you are both starting to believe me."

Cane, calmer now, turned to his partner and smiled. "What do you think? Are you starting to believe this fruitcake?"

Abell stared at Gabriel for several long and meaningful seconds before turning to his partner. "Let's go take a smoke break," he suggested, even though he had never smoked even once in his life.

*****

"You going to join me for a smoke?" Cane asked, incredulous.

Abell grinned. "No. I just wanted to bring the temperature in the room down a little. And I need another Diet-Coke."

"But that's not all, is it?"

"No. That's not all. Give me a few minutes to look something up before we go back in there."

"Take your time, Abell. Take all the time you need."

As Abell began to walk away, Cane called him back. "Wait a second. A while back, E.T. in there said that the desert where they did the Trinity test was ironically named."

"What of it?" Abell asked.

"You know that Spanish isn't one of the languages I speak. What's ironic about the . . . what did he call it? *Jornada del Muerto*?"

"*Jornada del Muerto* . . . the birthplace of the atomic bomb . . . translates into English as *Dead Man's Journey*, or the *Route of the Dead Man*. That's why it's ironic."

"*Gruszki na wierzbie*," Cane cursed, reaching for another cigarette. "This day just keeps getting better."

*****

"What's that one mean?" Abell asked once they had regathered outside of the sweat box.

"What's what one mean?"

"What you said earlier. It sounded like *Gretzky wants another beer*."

Cane laughed. "*Gruszki na wierzbie*. It means pears on a willow."

"I don't get it," Abell confessed. "Pears don't grow on willows; they grow on pear trees."

"That's the point. If someone gives you pears on a willow, then something is wrong; you're getting scammed. Just like he's doing to us in there."

"You really think so?"

"I don't know. He seems sincere enough. What do you think?"

"I think I can't wait for it to be Tuesday."

"Like Susanna Hoffs of *The Bangles* said, *It's just another manic Monday*," Cane teased as he went for another cigarette.

PART THREE

History Lessons

CHAPTER ELEVEN

"Are you familiar with Richard Hofstadter?" Abell asked his partner when they reconvened in the interrogation room.

Cane just shook his head, but Gabriel said, "As a matter of fact I am. What of him?"

Abell continued to examine the pages he had printed out before returning to the interrogation of their *suspect*. "Richard Hofstadter was a Pulitzer Prize winning author and historian. And in a 1964 essay of his, he was the first historian to analyze a new area of social studies which he called conspiracism."

Abell continued to leaf through the pages of Hofstadter's "The Paranoid Style in American Politics" essay before continuing. "He concluded that there seems to be a uniquely American need to assign blame for every great American tragedy, from Pearl Harbor to the Kennedy assassination. He went on to state that, if for every fluke accident or act of incompetence one can substitute an act of treason or an elaborate conspiracy, then those tragic events can make much more sense to the paranoid imagination of the American people."

"What's your point?" Cane asked.

"His point, Agent Canyon, is that it might be easy to dismiss my warnings as the rantings of a paranoid conspiracy theorist. However, there are several flaws in your theory, Agent Adamson."

"Enlighten me," Abell said.

"First, Mister Hofstadter died in 1970 and would not have been able to comment on much of what I am trying to tell you. Second, I am not an American. In fact, I am not even human. Therefore, I am not paralyzed by the uniquely American sense of political paranoia about which he wrote. Third, I am not a deranged black-helicopter-seeking, Oliver-Stone-worshipping, election -denying conspiracy theorist. As I have already demonstrated with the example of the *USS Akron* disaster, not every American tragedy is a result of the nefarious influence of my people. Other catastrophes, such as the 1986 explosion of your Space Shuttle *Challenger* or the terrorist attacks of September 11, 2001, are also just that. Catastrophes, but not conspiracies. Fourth, there are other countries in the world besides yours, and your people aren't the only ones who have suffered unspeakable tragedies. The nuclear meltdowns at Chernobyl and Fukushima, the Union Carbide chemical pesticide leak Bhopal, India, and the ammonium nitrate explosion in the Port of Beirut had nothing to do with the United States; however, they are all sufficient testament to the simple fact that your country does not have a monopoly on either tragedy or conspiracy theory. While not *all* of the misfortunes your people . . . and by, *your people*, I mean humans, not just Americans . . . have suffered over the past century or so are a direct result of actions on the part of my people, *many* of them are. But I called myself Gabriel because, like the angel of your Christian Bible, I am a messenger of good news."

"What good news is that?" Abell asked, unhappy at how easily he had been rebuked.

"That if you, or someone else like you, starts to take this threat seriously, then the next human tragedy can still be averted. That you might set aside your petty differences and antagonisms, realize how much unites all members of humanity, and turn your collective plowshares into swords, directed not against each other, but against the external enemy which threatens you all."

"And if we don't?"

"Then the next human tragedy will be your last one, and you will go the way of the dinosaurs!"

As Gabriel had been speaking, his voice had been rising—for the first time—in both tone and volume. When he was finished, an uneasy silence reigned momentarily in the interrogation room.

After agents Canyon and Adamson stared at him for several long seconds, Gabriel regained his composure and smiled. "Is it time for another cigarette break, Agent Canyon?"

*****

"Okay . . . okay," Cane began, without having taken another cigarette break. "Let's go with this. When did the alleged alien presence really begin?"

"As I said before, we've been sporadically monitoring things on this planet since the end of the nineteenth century, but our *continued* presence on this planet began on July 8, 1947."

"You know the exact date?" Abell asked in shock.

"Of course. That was the day when . . . according to official sources . . . something 'fell out of the sky' over Roswell, New Mexico. Almost immediately, however, your military recanted and claimed that what *fell from the sky* was simply a lost weather balloon."

"The military can't just recant something like that," Abell pointed out. "I was in the Air Force, and official statements have to come from *people . . .* commanding officers who . . ."

"Brigadier General Roger Maxwell Ramey," Gabriel interrupted.

"I beg your pardon."

"Brigadier. General. Roger. Maxwell. Ramey," Gabriel repeated, as if each word was its own complete sentence. "Well, technically, when he retired in 1957, he had reached the level of Lieutenant General, but he was a temporary Brigadier General in command of the Eighth Air Force in 1947. He was stationed at Fort Worth Army Airfield, which is now Carswell Air Force Base. In fact, there is a famous photograph of him taken on July 8, 1947, with a telex in his hand in which he reversed the military's stance on the nature of the craft that crashed in Roswell. As I explained earlier, we had taken notice of your advances earlier. But we didn't consider you an existential threat to our own survival until the three atomic explosions in the summer of 1945. The Roswell crash was an unfortunate result of our spying on your growing atomic capabilities."

"What happened to Ramey?" Abell asked.

Gabriel shot him a curious look. "Not that it really matters, but seven years later, in 1954, he was promoted to Lieutenant General and placed in command of the Fifth Air Force in Korea. He retired three years later and died in 1963, the same year as your President Kennedy."

"Whoa! You're saying that he had something to do with the Kennedy assassination?" Cane challenged.

"No, I am not. I'm simply answering your partner's question. After all, I am a suspect, am I not? Isn't that what I am supposed to do? You ask the questions and I answer them?"

After a lengthy silence, Abell asked, "So, what happened after Roswell?"

"There was a subsequent rash of what you might call *UFO sightings* in 1947. That's because, after the earlier crash, we heightened our surveillance of you. We were uncertain as to the nature of the crash, so we had to increase our surveillance."

"Then what? Assuming for a second that UFOs really were buzzing around the skies all over the place, our government must have responded in some way, right?" Cane asked.

"I would certainly say so," Gabriel answered. "You . . . *responded* . . . in a rather large way."

"Meaning what?" Abell inquired.

Gabriel took a deep breath before carrying on. "Your President Harry S. Truman signed the National Security Act into law on July 26, 1947. Less than three weeks after the so-called *Roswell Incident*."

"I'm afraid I'm not familiar with that particular piece of legislation," Cane confessed. "Could you please refresh my memory?"

"There must not be a movie about it," Abell mused aloud, teasing his partner.

Smiling, Gabriel explained: "Outside of the 2001 Patriot Act, it was only the most significant expansion and reorganization of the American military-industrial-complex in the nation's history. Among other provisions, it merged the Department of War and the Department of the Navy into a new and unified Department of Defense; it established a new Department of the Air Force as a separate branch of the National Military Establishment;

it created a new cabinet position called the Secretary of Defense; it created the National Security Council, *and* it established the Central Intelligence Agency. It was sort of a big deal."

"An act like that had to have been proposed long before the so-called Roswell Incident, *and* it would have been a logical and understandable way to further promote and protect the nation's security during the Cold War," Abell pointed out.

"Well done, Agent Adamson. That sounds like you quoted directly from Wikipedia, but your piercing analysis fails to include the idea that this legislation allowed for much greater coordination of the activities of your National Military Establishment with other departments and agencies of the federal government . . . as well as with private, civilian agencies—to say nothing of the fact that it also created Majestic 12, or MJ-12, a top-secret ad hoc intelligence committee with absolutely no congressional oversight. All of this a full two years before the Soviet Union successfully test-detonated its first atomic bomb. Something in the summer of 1947 scared President Truman to death, and it certainly wasn't the Russians."

"MJ-12?" Cane asked.

"The presence of aliens on this planet presented a potential military threat—a much greater one than that posed by the Soviet Union, by the way—which necessitated a massive buildup of secret money and technology, which were both to be kept far away from the scrutiny of the public as well as any oversight of your Congress. MJ-12 was the codename for a secret committee of scientists, military leaders, and government officials formed by a secret executive order. Its purpose was to coordinate and facilitate the investigation into and recovery of alien spacecraft and technology."

"Who's quoting from Wikipedia now?" Abell asked.

Before Gabriel could respond, Cane interjected. "I seem to remember something about that. It was some kind or urban legend that was first circulated by the Trekkies and UFO junkies in the 1980s. They claimed to have discovered a series of leaked secret government documents. But the FBI investigated and declared the documents to be completely bogus. Apparently, the whole thing was an elaborate hoax dreamed up by a bunch of Sci-Fi nerds. It's about as real as Big Foot or the Loch Ness fuckin' monster." Cane punctuated his comments by crossing his arms in a gesture of defiance and victory.

Gabriel simply smiled. "You knew of MJ-12, Agent Canyon. That's impressive. But do you also know of Otto von Bismarck?"

"The German statesman and diplomat?"

"Prussian, actually. But you have the gist of it."

"What of him?" Abell asked. "Are you going to tell us now that Bismarck was an alien?"

"No, don't be ridiculous, Agent Adamson. However, it was *Herr* Bismarck who famously maintained that one should never believe anything in politics until it has been officially denied. The best evidence that the extra-terrestrial threat to your people is quite real is the simple fact that your own employer . . . *the F. B. Fuckin' I* . . . says that it isn't real."

Feeling the full weight of Gabriel's taunt, Cane just glared at him.

Abell, on the other hand, smiled, showing that strange look once again that had earlier disturbed his partner.

CHAPTER TWELVE

As they made their way through the office, ostensibly on another cigarette/Diet-Coke break, Cane and his partner both demonstrated their exasperation with Gabriel, but in very different ways.

Abell, as was his custom, showed his by being very quiet.

Cane, as he did so often, cursed.

"Where does that nutcase in there get off making fun of me . . . and of the Bureau? He's really trying to get under my skin."

"Yep, and it seems like he's doing an excellent job," Abell mused.

"Yeah . . . whatever. What do we do with him now? I'm about fed up with all of this *Star Wars* crap."

"Let's go back in one more time before we decide what to do with him. But there's something else I want to look up first."

"Fine. There's something I want to look up, too. But if we don't charge him with something soon, we should just cut him loose. Agreed?"

"Agreed."

Cane and Abell went their separate ways.

Meanwhile, Gabriel just continued to wait.

*****

Before they reentered the interrogation room for what they hoped would be the final time, Cane and Abell literally compared notes.

"What do you got?" Cane asked his partner.

"Maybe nothing. You go first."

"Ugh, maybe nothing, too. But Mork from Ork in there really got me thinking, and I just spent the last hour compiling a list of things that our government initially denied but later had to admit to."

"Like?"

"Like the Tuskegee Syphilis Study conducted by the US Public Health Service in the 1930s and '40s which was finally exposed in the 1970s. Like the exchange of arms for hostages with Iran in the 1980s. Like the NSA's secret surveillance program that Eric Snowden exposed. Like the lies in 2003 about the Iraqi weapons of mass destruction that we now admit Saddam Hussein never had. Like the military's testing of chemical weapons on US civilians in San Francisco in the 1950s; that one, if you can believe it, was exposed by the Church of Scientology."

Showing an unusual level of anxiety and frustration, Cane continued to rifle through sheets of paper he had printed out. "Like the Gulf of Tonkin incident which really started our involvement in the Vietnam war, and which we finally admitted in 2005 never happened. Oh . . . and *Operation Paperclip*, which he mentioned earlier? It's all true. We denied it at first, of course, but we later admitted that was true. The list just goes on and on. The lies we concocted about the effects of marijuana; the truth about the toxicity of the dust at Ground Zero after 9/11; the truth about our involvement in the 1953 coup in Iran. The Kennedy assassinations. *Project Sunshine.* Watergate. The truth about Global Warming. In each and every case, some agency of our government swore categorically to the truth of something, only to later have to admit that it lied. And in each case, the truth came about as a result of some brave whistleblower or leaker who was initially dismissed as a nut or a conspiracy theorist."

"Just like our nutjob in there," Abell concluded.

"Exactly."

"Okay, but that's a long way from proving there's a massive conspiracy about an alien cover up."

Cane stared at his partner with a look of consternation Abell had never seen before.

"What?" Abell finally asked.

"Is it?"

"Is it what?"

"Is it that big of a leap?"

"I don't know. You tell me," Abell challenged.

Cane sighed heavily before continuing. "For years, the government swore that Area 51 never existed at all, even after it came to public attention in the 1950s. It took us until 2013, but we finally admitted that it is real. You still can't go there, of course; it's completely secure. But it's there. We admitted it. A highly classified government facility in the middle of the Mojave Desert, about one hundred miles north of Las Vegas, doing God-knows-what."

"Jesus!"

"Exactly. I'm not saying I believe our . . . resident alien . . . in there. But . . ."

"But what?" Abell asked.

"But it just seems to me that our government, including the Bureau itself, has a long and sordid history of telling lies and then standing behind those lies . . . even under the mounting pressure of overwhelming evidence to the contrary. But, eventually, some of their biggest lies have been exposed. So, what if that guy in there isn't just another crazed lunatic looking for attention? What if his story, which seems completely implausible . . . really isn't? What if he's telling the truth?"

The ominous portent of what Cane had just asked hung heavily in the air.

Finally Abell broke the silence. "Really makes you wonder, doesn't it?"

"About what?"

"About whether or not all of those crazy conspiracy theories about what the government put into the COVID vaccine really are true."

Cane hesitated just a moment before responding. "Well, if they are, we won't find out about it until around thirty years from now." He paused meaningfully before adding, "Fuck it. What do you have?"

It took Abell a few seconds to respond, but when he did he said, "Just something Gabriel said earlier. A reference he made to the . . . what was it?" Abell briefly consulted his notes. "To the *military industrial complex.*"

"Yeah—I know that one. It's from Eisenhower's farewell address. He gave it just days before he left office in 1961."

"How do you know that?" Abell asked, stunned.

"It was in the beginning of that Oliver Stone movie . . . *JFK*. Remember?"

"Jesus, I should have known you would have gotten it from a movie. And I just knew that Oliver Stone was going to show up one way or another before the day was out."

"So what? Why's that reference important?"

"That's what I want to find out. Let's go ask Gabriel. He seems to be the man with all of the answers anyway."

*****

As they sat back down, Gabriel asked for something for the first time. "Could I please have something to eat or drink? I haven't been offered anything since early yesterday, and while my physical needs are very different from yours, I do require some sustenance from time to time."

Cane and Abell stared at each other for a second. "Sure," Cane responded. "What do you want? Coffee? Doughnuts? Cigarettes? A candy bar?"

"A simple glass of water and something with some sodium in it will be sufficient," Gabriel responded.

"No sweat." Cane pushed his printed pages across the table to Gabriel. "Take a look at these while I'm gone."

After Cane left the room, Gabriel rifled through the sheets of paper and smiled. "It seems that your partner is starting to believe me."

As if he hadn't heard him, Abell simply began to read from his own printout. "Listen to this for a minute: *'We now stand ten years past the midpoint of a century that has witnessed four major wars among great nations. Three of these involved our own country. Despite these holocausts, America is today the strongest, the most influential and the most productive nation in the world. Understandably proud of this pre-eminence, we yet realize that America's leadership and prestige depend, not merely upon our unmatched material progress, riches and military strength, but on how we use our power in the interests of world peace and human betterment.'*

"'We face a hostile ideology—global in scope, atheistic in character, ruthless in purpose, and insidious in method. Unhappily, the danger it poses promises to be of indefinite duration.'

"'We have been compelled to create a permanent armaments industry of vast proportions. Added to this, three and a half million men and women are directly engaged in the defense establishment. We annually spend on military security alone more than the net income of all United States corporations. Now this conjunction of an immense military establishment and a large arms industry is new in the American experience. The total influence—economic, political, even spiritual—is felt in every city, every State house, every office of the Federal government.'

"'We must guard against the acquisition of unwarranted influence, whether sought or unsought, by the military-industrial complex. The potential for the disastrous rise of misplaced power exists and will persist. We must never let the weight of this combination endanger our liberties or democratic processes.'"

"Yes?" Gabriel said. "Is that it?"

"Do you recognize that speech?"

"Yes, I do. It was delivered by your President Eisenhower on television on January 17, 1961 . . . just three days before he left office."

"What do you think about it?"

"What do I think about it?"

"Yes. You mentioned the term military-industrial complex earlier, so I was just wondering what you thought about Eisenhower's speech about it."

"What I think about it," Gabriel mused aloud. "Well, I think that men like CIA Director Allen Dulles, CIA Deputy Director for Plans Richard Bissel, CIA Deputy Director General Charles Cabel, and Special Assistant to the President for Foreign Affairs Nelson Rockefeller did the work in the 1950s that created the very military-industrial complex that Eisenhower warned about in this daring speech. I also believe that it is not a coincidence that Eisenhower waited until just before he left office to make that speech."

"Why is that?" Abell interrupted.

"Because Eisenhower, a man well-schooled in military tactics, was wise enough to fear these four men. I think it is very unfortunate that his successor, President Kennedy, did not fear those four fanatical cold warriors as much as Eisenhower obviously did. If he had, perhaps he would have lived longer."

"Eisenhower?"

"No, Kennedy. But that's not really what you wanted to ask me is it?"

"No, it is not."

"Go ahead and ask your question."

Abell paused and then, without even consulting his notes, asked, "When Eisenhower mentioned *'a hostile ideology—global in scope, atheistic in character, ruthless in purpose, and insidious in method,'* he wasn't talking about the Soviet Union was he?"

"No, he was not. Nor was he talking about the broader global threat of monolithic Communism, which never really existed, by the way."

"What, then, was he referring to?"

"Agent Adamson, I think we both know precisely what Mister Eisenhower was talking about."

*****

When he reentered the room with a bottle of water and a small bag of pretzels, Cane could immediately tell that something had changed. During his brief departure from the room, something significant had happened in his absence. Specifically, a new dynamic seemed to exist between Gabriel and Agent Adamson.

Handing the water and pretzels across the table, Cane asked, "What's up? What are we talking about?"

Abell said nothing, and Gabriel waited several seconds before he finally said, "I believe we were talking about President Eisenhower, weren't we?"

CHAPTER THIRTEEN

Gabriel, who had begun to look ashen and sleepy, took a few sips of water and ate two of the pretzels provided by Agent Canyon and seemed instantly refreshed. His eyes, which had been heavy mere moments earlier, now blazed with new acuity and purpose, causing Cane to wonder for just a moment how strange it must feel to be suspended above the physical needs of human beings. Then, shaking his head in disbelief of his own craziness, he turned towards his partner and saw that he was as impassive as he had been upon their arrival in the office that morning, his perceptions stored away behind a cold veneer of professionalism.

Arrayed in front of Cane was a set of papers that appeared to bear a printout of Eisenhower's farewell address from 1961. After picking up the pages and glancing briefly at them, he attempted to reinitiate the strange conversation. "Eisenhower, huh? What about him?"

Gabriel stared awkwardly at Abell for several moments before beginning again. "In July of 1952, what you call UFOs were buzzing around your nation's capital, and your President Harry Truman was powerless to do anything about it. Whether he was unwilling, or simply unable, to confront this significant and emerging new threat during his waning time in office is irrelevant. What does matter is that he simply did nothing. However, he was soon replaced . . ."

"*. . . succeeded . . .*" Abell interrupted. "There's a difference."

"Very well. He was *succeeded* in January of 1953 by President Eisenhower—a former general, and a man used to assessing and destroying military threats. But Mister Eisenhower also knew that the key to defeating an enemy—any enemy, whether it was the Nazis, the Communists, or visitors from another planet—is knowing more than your opponent. In *The Art of War*, Sun Tzu said that all warfare is based upon deception. There's tremendous truth to that, but Sun Tzu is incomplete, and General Eisenhower . . ."

"*. . . President* Eisenhower . . ." Abell interrupted again, causing a questioning look to cross his partner's face.

What's going on with him? Cane wondered. *Why does he keep getting hung up on semantics?*

"But *Mister* Eisenhower," Gabriel emphasized, refusing to make a concession a second time, "also knew that, in modern warfare, intelligence and counterintelligence were the ultimate keys to deception. And he simply didn't have enough intelligence to determine the level of this new threat to your nation."

"So?" Cane asked. "What did he do about it? Did he take a trip to your planet?"

"No," Gabriel responded sincerely. "But he did meet with some of my people . . . ones who had made a trip to yours."

*****

"Say that again, please."

Gabriel smiled. "I have noticed, Agent Canyon, that your manners have improved substantially as we have progressed today. That seems to me to be an indicator of your increasing level of belief in the veracity of my claims."

Cane just smirked. "Just keep going . . . *please.*"

"In 1954 . . . very few people know this . . . in just his second year in office, your President Eisenhower actually had a face-to-face meeting with captured members of my people at Muroc Air Force Base in California."

"*Muroc?*" Cane asked, confused, looking towards Abell—a veteran of the Air Force. "There's no such base, is there?"

"There was in 1954," Abell confirmed. "It was renamed Edwards Air Force Base in honor of pilot Captain Glen Edwards who was killed in a crash when test-flying a Northrop YB-49, the all-jet version of the Flying Wing bomber."

"Yes, that is correct, Agent Adamson."

"But Edwards died in 1948," Abell pointed out, showing some pride at having caught Gabriel in an obvious error. "And the base was renamed in his honor in December of the following year . . . 1949—a full five years *before* the alleged meeting between Ike and *your people.* So there could not have been a meeting at Muroc Air Force Base in 1954 between President Eisenhower and any aliens . . . or anyone else, for that matter."

"Quite right again, Agent Adamson. It *was* Edwards Air Force Base when the meeting took place in 1954. But, as I stated earlier, my people crashed on this planet in 1947, and when they were imprisoned at that facility, it was still *Muroc* Air Force Base. Shall I continue?"

A dark scowl passed over Abell's face, and Cane again noticed the altered dynamic between the partner he'd known for years and the suspect he'd only known since that morning.

"Go ahead. Keep going," Cane encouraged.

"Very well. At that 1954 meeting, your President Eisenhower was urged by my people . . . his prisoners, effectively . . . to cease nuclear weapons development. Obviously, *Ike,* as you called him, declined."

"Obviously," Cane echoed.

"Instead, he signed a top-secret executive memorandum, National Security Memo 5510, which made the previously established Majestic 12 a permanent national security committee, separate from and above all other existing national security agencies. Its purpose was, and still is, to oversee and conduct all covert activities concerned with the alien presence here on Earth."

Gabriel could see that Cane was about to interrupt, but he headed him off. "And, yes, Agent Canyon, the FBI, the very agency which employs you, has publicly and officially denounced the very existence of MJ-12; however, as you can clearly see from all of these pages you printed here, governments in general—and yours in particular—are often quick to deny the existence of things they find difficult to explain. I mean, before today, could you have believed that your Atomic Energy Commission was capable of conducting a series of studies which required them to procure 1,500 cadavers—many of them belonging to babies and young children, and many of them taken without their parents' knowledge or consent—all in an attempt to ascertain the impact of radioactive fallout on the world's population? But now you know that it did—all in the name of national security."

"What's he talking about?" asked an astonished Abell.

"*Project Sunshine.* I told you about it before. He's telling the truth . . . at least about that one."

"There's no way!" Abell asserted demonstratively. "Our government doesn't do things like that!"

"I'm afraid it's quite true, Agent Adamson. The program began in 1954, the same year that President Eisenhower encountered my people for the first time. And, not for nothing, but the program that *Project Sunshine* built off of actually began several years earlier with a series of studies regarding the formation, transformation, fallout, and biological hazards associated with atomic bomb debris. Those studies were supported by a global policy think tank founded in 1948 by the Douglas Aircraft Company and financed by your government to offer research and analysis to the United States military following World War Two. That research institute is called the RAND Corporation, and the top-secret study it was conducting was codenamed *Project Gabriel.* You simply cannot make this stuff up."

"Okay, we seem to have deviated pretty far off course here," Cane pointed out. "Let's get back to the alleged meeting between Eisenhower and the . . . I still can't believe I'm saying this . . . the aliens."

"What of it?"

"Why would Eisenhower, or MJ-12, or the CIA . . . why would any of them want to keep the discovery of an alien presence here on Earth a secret?" Abell asked. "What I mean is, if the creation of a military-industrial whatever was so important to these . . . what did you call them? *Fanatical cold warriors?* Then why not simply disclose the truth? Wouldn't that provide the public with ample incentive to support a massive military buildup?"

Gabriel didn't even hesitate before responding. "Isn't it obvious, Agent Adamson? The public could not be told because a full disclosure of life on other planets—to say nothing of the fact that said life was hostile to humans—would almost certainly lead to an overnight collapse of religious and financial institutions, culminating in complete social disorder and near-total anarchy. In fact, secrecy was so paramount that not even Congress could know, which meant that funding had to come from . . . *untraditional* . . . government financial sources."

"What exactly are *untraditional* government financial sources?" Cane asked.

"Things like the massive amount of gold seized from Japanese General Tomoyuki Yamashita at the end of World War Two."

"What?"

Gabriel exhaled deeply. "Why is it that Americans do not bother to learn even their own history anymore? Anyway, towards the end of World War Two, President Truman authorized *Operation Golden Lily*, a plunder of the war treasure that General Tomoyuki Yamashita had hidden in caves north of Manila in the Philippines."

"How much could that have amounted to?" Abell asked skeptically.

"According to several conservative estimates, the gold and gems seized from over two-hundred locations in the Philippines would have been worth more than one-hundred billion dollars." Gabriel paused for emphasis, allowing that dollar figure to hang in the air for a moment. "Is it time for another Diet-Coke, Agent Adamson?" he finally asked.

"Wait a minute? What kind of things would this MJ-12 need one-hundred billion dollars for?" Cane asked.

"Well, according to several reliable sources, also present at that 1954 meeting between your president and my people was the closest thing your country had to a modern-day Leonardo da Vinci—a man named Howard Hughes. Through his genius and his connections with companies like the Lockheed Corporation, you were able to reverse engineer the technology of our crashed vehicle into ambitious projects like Lockheed's U2 spy plane program, as well as the RAND Corporation's CORONA spy satellite network, both of which were allegedly designed to keep a better eye on the Soviets after the launch of *Sputnik*. In reality, however, both programs—which would have been impossible without the technology from the vehicle that crashed in Roswell—were really designed to keep a better eye on us."

"One-hundred billion dollars is a lot of money, but it hardly sounds like enough to support massive programs like the U2 spy plane or the CORONA spy satellites for an indefinite period of time," Abell pointed out.

"Quite right. Top marks again, Agent. But *Operation Golden Lily* was only one such source of off-the-record revenue. There were others."

"Such as?" Cane wanted to know.

"Such as the illegal drug market which your government has cornered since the 1950s."

Neither Cane nor Abell seemed at all shocked by this revelation. In fact, they shared a look of complicity when they glanced briefly at each other.

"I see this comes as no surprise to either of you two gentlemen. I suppose it's nothing to be ashamed of; after all, the British and the French had established ample precedent for this with the Opium Wars of the nineteenth century. Those wars gave them political control over China and Indochina, just as your so-called "war on drugs" has given you economic control of some of the most impoverished parts of the world today. But let's not get into that just now. We'd end up going round and round talking about George Herbert Walker "Poppy" Bush; his father, Prescott Bush; the Bush family's interests in Texas oil, eastern banks, and the American intelligence apparatus; Zapata Oil; the illegal use of drug sales to support the Contras in Nicaragua; the connections between the Bush family and the Saudi government, and all sorts of other unsavory details—very little of which is germane to our reason for meeting."

Eager to not have to replough the embarrassing ground of America's criminal and already well-documented involvement in the international drug trade, Cane leapt at the opportunity Gabriel had just provided.

"Fine. Let's go back to *Sputnik* then," he advised.

"Very well. Despite your advances in atomic and nuclear technology, it wasn't really until the Soviets launched *Sputnik* in 1957 that we began to intervene in global affairs more actively—taking part in things like the Bay of Pigs Invasion, the Cuban Missile Crisis, and both of the Kennedy assassinations. Our aim, of course, was to exploit your fear of the Soviet Union and the Russians' innate paranoia about the West to get the two of you to wage war against each other. If we could somehow trigger the two so-called "superpowers" to wage nuclear war against each other, well . . . you'd no longer pose a threat to us—or anyone else, for that matter."

Abell sighed in disbelief. "You lied before, Gabriel. You really do love Oliver Stone, don't you? Are you now claiming that a secret alien conspiracy is responsible for the failure of the Bay of Pigs invasion *and* the assassination of President Kennedy?" Abell looked toward his partner and rolled his eyes with the last comment.

"And why is that so hard to believe, Agent Adamson? We've been compromising your very systems of government and defense since the 1950s. Why do you think Redstone and your early space program were both met with such massive failure? Why do you suppose so many of your leaders met untimely and unfortunate ends? I have been trying to tell you for several hours now that we are not benevolent alien beings who have come to enlighten or befriend you. Since the 1950s, we have learned to fear you; as a result, we have become compelled to at least cripple, if not completely eradicate, your entire civilization. And the completion of those efforts is as certain as the temperature at which water boils. Why have you not been paying attention?"

Suddenly remembering something that Gabriel had said earlier, Cane chimed back in. "Wait a second. Earlier, you said that your people have done *almost* everything in your power to sabotage the advancement of our technology."

"That's correct, Agent Canyon. *Almost* everything."

"What's the one thing in your power that you haven't yet tried?" Cane asked hesitantly, fearing that he already knew the answer.

"We have not invaded your planet, Agent Canyon. Not yet, at least."

CHAPTER FOURTEEN

"Okay," Abell said, rubbing his eyes and attempting to restart the conversation. "Let's shelve the whole alien invasion thing for a second and get back to where we were before, okay?"

"Very well, Agent Adamson. What would you like to know now?"

"So, after a half century or so of just observing and occasionally meddling, all of your . . . more *active* intervention . . . really took off during the Eisenhower years, huh? Is that just unfortunate timing for Ike, or did your people have some specific reason to pick on him? Was it his superior golf skills that threatened you?"

"Actually, superior golf skills notwithstanding, Eisenhower wasn't nearly as important, nor as threatening, to my people as his Vice-president was," Gabriel assured the two agents.

"Nixon?" Cane asked. "Now that I can believe. If Nixon were caught up in an alien conspiracy, or even if he were one himself, that would explain a lot."

Gabriel smiled, but Cane's partner did not.

"I hate to disappoint you, Agent Canyon, but Richard Milhous Nixon was not an alien. However, as a former naval officer, a two-term Congressman and member of the House Un-American Activities Committee, a United States Senator for three years, and Eisenhower's Vice-president for eight, he had established himself as a major player in the military industrial complex and was as "plugged in" as anyone ever, with the possible exception of George H. W. Bush. As a result, we took several steps to ensure that he did *not* become President when Eisenhower left office in 1961. His opponent, Massachusetts Senator John F. Kennedy, appeared to be a much less significant threat to us than Richard Nixon, so we made sure that Kennedy won."

"Here we go," Abell groaned. "The sorry old Chicago voter conspiracy again. So you're now going to tell us that all of the dead people in Chicago who voted for Kennedy in 1960 were actually aliens."

"No, of course not. However, we did begin to derail Mister Nixon's campaign long before the election in November of 1960. In fact, our efforts began as early as May 1, 1960."

"What happened on May 1, 1960?" Cane asked.

"That was the day when the Soviet Union allegedly shot down Francis Gary Powers as he was conducting an illegal surveillance flight over the Soviet Union."

"Allegedly?"

"Yes. The Soviets could not have possibly shot down a U2 plane that they couldn't even detect on radar. And if they did somehow manage to shoot it out of the sky with a missile, then how do you explain how much of the plane hit the ground intact? The Soviets didn't shoot down anything; we did. It was an EMP burst from one of our vessels. The whole purpose of your U2 program wasn't to spy on the Russians, it was to send a loud and clear message to my people that it was the United States, and not the Soviet Union, which was the dominant technological power in the world at the time. In fact, just one year earlier, Mister Nixon nearly said as much during his famous "Kitchen Debate" with Soviet leader Nikita Khrushchev. It was at that time, while Nixon and his wife were visiting Moscow in July of 1959, that one of our people who was assigned to the Spaso House, that's the US ambassador's residence in Spasopeskovskaya Square, exposed him to a dose of ionizing radiation. Your Secret Service finally disclosed that fact just last year. At the time it happened, they denied it, of course; but they have finally revealed the true story—in a sense, anyway. They're still desperately clinging to the ridiculous cover story that the failed attempt was made by the Soviets."

"You exposed Richard Nixon . . ."

". . . and his wife . . ."

". . . *and his wife* . . . to radiation while they were in Moscow in 1959?"

"Yes."

"For what purpose?" Cane asked.

"To kill him, of course. Obviously, however, the plan failed, so we were forced to employ other means of eliminating him as a potential threat."

"Such as?" Cane responded.

"Such as the U2 incident. It was our hope that one of two things would happen when we knocked that plane down over Soviet airspace. Either, the incident would provoke a thermonuclear war between the United States and the Soviet Union, or the embarrassment of the incident and the subsequent bungled cover-up would cripple Nixon politically. Eisenhower was already on his way out of office at the time, but Nixon still had a bright future ahead of him."

Cane and Abell stared dumbfounded at Gabriel. Seeing that no additional questions were forthcoming, he decided to proceed on his own. "In the summer of 1960, shortly after the U2 incident, while serving as chairman of the National Security Council's "Special Group," or 5412 committee, which oversaw covert activities, Mister Nixon contacted famed aircraft designer and business tycoon, as well as Eisenhower confidante, Howard Hughes. In a deranged and misguided attempt at revenge for the U2 incident, the two attempted to arrange for the assassination of Cuban dictator Fidel Castro, but they desired to do so without leaving any US fingerprints on the mission. Despite constant rumors of mental instability, Hughes was actually a brilliant and powerful master of multiple defense-related industries, as well as one of Nixon's secret donors. So he agreed; and to ensure the success of this Castro mission, Nixon and Hughes sought out the assistance of both your mafia and the CIA. Codenamed *Operation Zapata*—Zapata, by the way, being the name of the Bush family's Texas oil company—this effort culminated in the failed Bay of Pigs invasion, a near fatal political disaster for President Kennedy."

After several seconds of stunned silence, Abell finally recovered enough to ask, "What, in the world, does any of this have to do with little green men?"

Gabriel smiled. "First of all, Agent Adamson, I am familiar with life forms on multiple different planets, and I can assure you that none of them are green; nor are they men, for that matter. Most of us are colored a sort of muted gray and are, by your human definitions, gender neutral."

"I just knew there was going to be an LGBTQ connection here somewhere," Cane groaned.

Gabriel looked briefly confused. "While I am not at all familiar with that particular agency, I can assure you that, if it had any meaningful political power, Richard Nixon was LGBTQ from the very beginning."

For the first time all morning, both Cane and Abell erupted in laughter.

"And I always thought it was J. Edgar Hoover who was a little light in the loafers," Cane chortled. "Okay, I owe you one, Gabriel. That comment alone made this morning's . . . whatever this is . . . worthwhile."

Looking perplexed, Gabriel responded, "I don't understand what could possibly be funny about any of this. If Mister Nixon were morally and logistically capable of covertly arranging for the attempted assassination of another foreign leader, then how much more capable and willing would he be to wage hostile action against my people? That's why we had to ensure that he did not win the election in 1960. How else can you explain the fact that the most politically experienced and most recognized man of his generation lost to a political novice and a relative nobody like John Kennedy? That would be like . . ."

"Like Hillary Clinton losing to an assclown like Trump?" Cane offered helpfully,

"Precisely! While I do not know what an assclown is, Kennedy's apparent defeat of Nixon was as shocking as Mister Trump's alleged victory over Secretary of State Clinton in 2016. And it would not have been possible without direct interference from my people."

"Which one?" Abell asked.

"I beg your pardon."

"Which one wouldn't have been possible without alien election interference? Kennedy's win over Nixon in 1960, or Clinton's loss to Trump in 2016."

"Both."

*****

After yet another cigarette/Diet-Coke break, during which Gabriel finished his water and pretzels, Cane and Abell returned to the interrogation room and started again.

"Okay," Abell began. "Setting aside your failed assassination attempt against Nixon, as well as your failed attempt to ruin him politically by shooting down a U2 spy plane over the Soviet Union, how were you able to manage rigging the 1960 election in Kennedy's favor?"

Gabriel sat back in his chair and crossed his arms as if insulted by the mendacity of Abell's question. "Are you serious, Agent Adamson? Your country invented and adopted mechanical lever voting machines in the late nineteenth century; and by the middle of the twentieth century, the era of electronic vote counting had begun. Once you had eschewed paper ballot counting for machine counts, it became mere child's play for us to predetermine the counts. Literally, child's play. A newly hatched infant of but eight weeks on my planet is capable of both accessing and compromising your voting records."

"Right now, Rudy Guliani and Sidney Powell are somewhere saying 'I knew it!'," Cane laughed.

"Yeah—probably from prison. And don't forget that crazy pillow guy. If there really are aliens living on this planet, he's got to be one of them."

"No doubt about it. In fact, he . . . wait a minute."

"Here it comes," Gabriel predicted.

Just now catching on, Abell added, "Did you just say a newly *hatched* infant?"

Gabriel smiled. "I was wondering how long it would take the two of you to catch up to that. Yes, my people are neither procreated nor birthed through the same disgusting process as your people. I tried to discuss it with you earlier, but . . ."

Cane closed his eyes and vigorously shook his head while Abell kept saying, "No. No. No. We are *not* going there."

Gabriel, obviously reveling in the agents' discomfort, just continued to smile. "Very well then. But I'm ready to resume your . . . *interrogation* . . . whenever you are."

"Okay. Okay. Okay," Cane kept repeating, trying to erase from his mind the visual image of Gabriel emerging from an egg. "Okay, so you rigged the

1960 election, right? Because it's child's play, and because Nixon posed a bigger threat to you than Kennedy, right? So then what?"

"Less than one month after Kennedy's inauguration, more than fifty of our vessels . . . what you call UFOs . . . invaded the skies over Europe. Despite the fact that they flew very high and very fast, they were visible to your NATO radar stations. We always began by flying west out of Soviet airspace; then crossed over Poland, East Germany, West Germany, and northern France; then flew over Great Britain, and ultimately disappeared from NATO radar somewhere over Norway."

"Why?"

"Why what, Agent Adamson?"

"Why fly those sorties, and why always the same flight path?"

"For two reasons, actually. First, we *wanted* you to be able to see us. If we didn't want to be seen by your radar . . . well, then, we wouldn't. The second reason is that we were, once again, trying to provoke you and the Soviet Union into a destructive war. Whenever our vessels appeared in the skies over Europe, the Soviets thought they belonged to you, and you thought they belonged to the Soviets, which was precisely the point. And on February 2, 1961, we almost succeeded. In the opening days of the Kennedy presidency, we very nearly provoked a catastrophic war between East and West. This, too, was covered up for many years. But, despite our initial failure, the threat of accidental nuclear war remained an existential threat to the survival of the human race, and we were the proximate cause of that threat."

"Wait a minute," Cane called out, referring to his notes. Abell couldn't believe that his partner was actually taking notes on this garbage. "Let's get back to the Bay of Pigs invasion . . . *Operation Zapata*, or whatever you called it."

Inwardly pleased that he seemed to be getting somewhere with Agent Canyon, Gabriel smiled and said, "Yes? What of it?"

"You said earlier that it was the culmination of a Nixon plan to assassinate Castro. With help from Howard Hughes, right?"

"Yes."

"But the invasion didn't happen until April of 1961."

"April 17th through 20th, to be precise."

"Right. But Kennedy was president by then."

"Correct again."

"So why didn't he stop it?"

"Now we are getting somewhere, Agent Canyon," Gabriel praised. "Despite Kennedy's election, the intelligence community's plans for the Bay of Pigs invasion continued, without either the president's knowledge or consent. And by the time he was made aware of it, it was too late to stop it. Not that he didn't try, however. When the plan was first presented to him, just weeks after he took the oath of office, he initially disapproved of it. However, throughout the 1960 campaign, he had repeatedly called for American intervention in Cuba and had run to the right of Nixon as an anti-communist hawk. In fact, he regularly beat up President Eisenhower for allowing Castro to come to power in the first place. So, he felt boxed in, in large part because he didn't want to appear to be a soft-on-communism hypocrite. Ultimately, as I'm sure you both know, the mission was folly. It failed in every way, shape, and form. Although he publicly accepted blame for the failure, behind closed doors, Kennedy blamed the CIA and began a war with them which ultimately cost both him and his brother their lives."

"All of that because of Castro and Cuba?" Cane asked. "You're claiming that there's a straight line between Nixon, Howard Hughes, the Bay of Pigs Invasion, and the Kennedy assassinations?"

"I'll go you one better, Agent Canyon. A decade later, that tragedy still haunted American political leaders. In fact, the primary reason for the bungled Watergate break-in of 1972 had nothing to do with "digging up dirt" on George McGovern. Nixon knew he was going to win in a landslide in 1972 anyway. The reason for that burglary was that Nixon wanted to retrieve sensitive documents, which were in the possession of the Democratic party, that implicated him, and the CIA, and the mafia in an elaborate and, ultimately unsuccessful, plot to murder Fidel Castro."

Abell sighed unusually loudly. "Okay. A lot of this is just your typical conspiracy theorist's wet dream. But I will admit that, while there's a lot of smoke there, there is some . . . *some* . . . fire. But even if all of this is true, and I'm not saying that any of it is, what does it have to do with aliens?"

"I know this all seems impossible to believe, Agent Adamson, but do me a favor. Consult your internet. Look up the speech that President Kennedy gave to the American Newspaper Association just one week after the Bay of Pigs invasion. Then come back and tell me what you think. Most people who heard the speech thought he was referring to the monolithic and ruthless Communist plot for world domination—a sort of hawkish, get-tough-on-the-Reds diatribe designed to rehabilitate his image as a hardened cold warrior after the first significant foreign policy debacle of his young presidency. I think, however, if you view it critically, in light of what you now know to be true, you will see it with new eyes and hear it with new ears. I'll be waiting right here when you're done."

CHAPTER FIFTEEN

*"M*y topic tonight is a more sober one, of concern to publishers as well as editors. I want to talk about our common responsibilities in the face of a common danger. The events of recent weeks may have helped to illuminate that challenge for some, but the dimensions of its threat have loomed large on the horizon for many years."*

"You think he's talking about Cuba?" Cane asked as he and his partner huddled over a laptop on his desk. As Gabriel had suggested, they had opened YouTube and were watching a video of the speech that President Kennedy had given to the American Newspaper Association one week after the failed Bay of Pigs invasion.

"I don't know. Let's listen some more."

"Whatever our hopes may be for the future, for reducing this threat, or living with it, there is no escaping either the gravity or the totality of its challenge to our survival and to our security, a challenge that confronts us in unaccustomed ways in every sphere of human activity. This deadly challenge imposes upon our society two requirements of direct concern, both to the press and to the president. Two requirements that may seem almost contradictory in tone, but which must be reconciled and fulfilled if we are to meet this national peril.

"I refer first to the need for far greater public information, and second, to the need for far greater official secrecy. The very word secrecy is repugnant

in a free and open society, and we are as a people, inherently and historically, opposed to secret societies, to secret oaths, and to secret proceedings. We decided long ago that the dangers of excessive and unwarranted conceal-ment of pertinent facts far outweigh the dangers which are cited to justify it. Even today, there is little value in opposing the threat of a closed society by imitating its arbitrary restrictions. Even today, there is little value in ensuring the survival of our nation if our traditions do not survive with it. And there is very grave danger that an announced need for increased security will be seized upon by those anxious to expand its meaning to the very limits of official censorship and concealment. That I do not intend to permit to the extent that it's in my control, and no official of my administration, whether his rank is high or low, civilian or military, should interpret my words here tonight as an excuse to censor the news, to stifle dissent, to cover up our mistakes, or to withhold from the press and the public the facts they deserve to know."

The audience on the video began to clap vigorously, and Abell began to talk over the clip. "This doesn't seem to have anything to do with anything," he pointed out, seemingly eager to move along. "Let's fast forward a bit."

But just as Abell reached for the laptop, Cane grabbed his hand to stop him. "Hang on a second. I want to hear the rest of this."

"Today, no war has been declared, and however fierce the struggle may be, it may never be declared in the traditional fashion. Our way of life is under attack. Those who make themselves our enemy are advancing around the globe. The survival of our friends is in danger, and yet no war has been declared, no borders have been crossed by marching troops, no missiles have been fired. If the press is awaiting a declaration of war, before it imposes the self-discipline of combat conditions, then I can only say that no war ever posed a greater threat to our security. If you are awaiting a finding of clear and present danger, then I can only say that the danger has never been more clear, and its presence has never been more imminent."

"He's clearly talking about the Commies," Abell said, dismissively. "That nutcase Gabriel is just jerking our chains."

But Cane continued to listen carefully anyway.

"It requires a change in outlook, a change in tactics, a change in missions by the government, by the people, by every businessman or labor leader, and by every newspaper. For we are opposed around the world by a monolithic and ruthless conspiracy that relies primarily on covert means for expanding its fear of

influence, on infiltration instead of invasion, on subversion instead of elections, on intimidation instead of free choice, on guerrillas by night instead of armies by day. It is a system which has conscripted vast human and material resources into the building of a tightly knit, highly efficient machine that combines military, diplomatic, intelligence, economic, scientific, and political operations. Its preparations are concealed, not published . . ."

As the speech continued for another nine minutes, Cane looked up from his laptop and stared in disbelief at his partner.

"What?" Abell asked.

"Christ! Didn't you listen? He's not talking about the Commies. He's talking about a fuckin' alien conspiracy to infiltrate and overthrow our society."

"No way! Don't let Buck Rogers in there start getting to you; you're too smart for that."

Cane manipulated the cursor on the laptop and rewound the video to the 8:57 mark and let it replay for forty-four seconds. For the second time in just a few minutes, Abell heard President Kennedy call out the following warning: *"Our way of life is under attack. Those who make themselves our enemy are advancing around the globe. The survival of our friends is in danger, and yet no war has been declared, no borders have been crossed by marching troops, no missiles have been fired. If the press is awaiting a declaration of war, before it imposes the self-discipline of combat conditions, then I can only say that no war ever posed a greater threat to our security. If you are awaiting a finding of clear and present danger, then I can only say that the danger has never been more clear, and its presence has never been more imminent."*

Cane then held up one of the pages Abell had printed out earlier and read aloud from the text of Eisenhower's farewell address. *"We face a hostile ideology—global in scope, atheistic in character, ruthless in purpose, and insidious in method. Unhappily, the danger it poses promises to be of indefinite duration.'* Can you honestly tell me that, after everything he has told us in there today, that you don't see a connection here?" Cane's voice, both in volume and tone, attracted some attention from others in the office.

"Whoa there, cowboy!" Abell said, backing up slightly and raising his hands in a gesture of mock surrender. "You're not starting to drink Gabriel's Kool-Aid now, are you?"

"Don't be an asshole. You know I'm easily duped by a snake oil salesman."

"But . . . ?"

"But a lot of what he's said in there checks out, and the connections that he's making, well . . ."

"Well what?"

"Well, they just connect is all. Eisenhower and Kennedy, who couldn't agree on anything, are basically saying the same God-damned thing!"

Looking around the office to see if they still had an audience, Abell leaned back in towards where his partner was perched over his laptop and whispered, "Listen, Cane, just because Flash Gordon in there has gotten lucky on a few dates doesn't mean he's dealing with a full deck. And, okay, some of his crazier stories have been confirmed by what's on that vast cultural wasteland known as the internet, but that's still light years . . . sorry, no pun intended . . . from credibility."

Cane's shoulders sank in defeat. "You really think he's nuts, don't you?"

"I do."

"And now you think I'm nuts because I'm starting to believe him."

"No, I think you're tired, that's all. That damn Strunk case took a lot more out of you than it did me. He had us running in circles for months. When's the last time you've had more than four straight hours of sleep?"

"Sleep is for the weak," Cane responded.

"Maybe, but sleep is also for the dead. And if you don't get some soon, that's where you're going to end up. Dead."

Abell looked around the office again before continuing. "Why don't you take a short break? Let me go back in there and try to crack that nut. If I do, great. If I don't, then you come back in and we finish up together."

"If you don't believe any of this, then why go back in there at all?"

Abell made quite a show of pretending to be deep in thought. "Well, I just can't wait to see what he comes up with when we get to the Kennedy assassination. You know that I love that stuff almost as much as you do."

"Hey! Don't do that one without me. I want to know if it was Oswald or aliens on the grassy knoll."

"Oh, I'm sure he'll tell us. But I promise that I'll wait. In the meantime, go get some lunch, lay off the coffee and cigarettes for a bit, and we'll check back with each other in about an hour or so. Deal?"

"Deal."

Little did Abell know that his "permission" to let his partner go off on his own for an hour was precisely what Cane had hoped would happen.

*****

"What's the matter, *Double A*?" Robert West asked as Abell walked past his desk. "Lover's quarrel between you and the big guy?"

Abell couldn't stand Agent West. He was the kind of asshole who thought he was smarter than everyone else in the office when, in reality, he was living proof that cousins shouldn't procreate. Worse, however, than his inflated sense of intelligence was his perception of his sense of humor. The problem was that he thought he had one.

He was wrong.

But before Abell could offer anything by way of a response, Edward Schneider—an older agent who was now deskbound but whom Abell had come to respect and admire due to his legendary and incomparable work ethic—said, without even looking up from his work, "Hey, Bob. How did your surgery go last week?"

"What surgery?" West asked, blindly stepping into Schneider's trap.

"You know, the one where the doctors removed your head from your ass. Or did they decide to just leave it up there?"

Silenced once again by a rebuke from "the old guy," West fumed and made his way back to his desk to occupy himself with whatever it was that he did when he wanted to make it look like he was actually doing some work.

Abell and Schneider exchanged a smile and a knowing glance as they went about their business. But as Abell made his way back towards the sweat box, Agent Schneider called out to him. "Hey, *Ack Ack*. Come by and see me later. I got a good one for you. Did you hear the joke about Hurricane Beulah?"

"Let me guess," Abell responded. "It will *blow* me away."

"Nah, but it's worth thirty seconds."

"Yeah, I'll catch you later. First I have to go see an alien about a horse."

PART FOUR

Moon Shot

CHAPTER SIXTEEN

"Where's Agent Canyon?" Gabriel asked when Abell reentered the interrogation room alone.

"He's . . . on a break."

"Oh," Gabriel responded, a knowing look on his face.

"What am I missing? Why is that amusing to you?"

"Well, I'm assuming that you're now going to begin the "good-cop-bad-cop" part of our little play here."

Now it was Abell's turn to smile. "No. First of all, you always want to start with the bad cop and then bring in the good cop. And if anyone is the bad cop here, it's Agent Canyon. Second, that's not what we're doing anyway."

"Good, because that would not pay any dividends."

"Why? Because you're too tough to crack? Let me tell you something, *Gabriel*, I've cracked a lot tougher nuts than you. We just came off the Strunk case where we met a pair of guys named Prem and Reynolds, and those three were the toughest bastards I've ever come across. But eventually, they sang, too. They all do. It's just a matter of time."

"No, Agent Adamson. While I do not know who Strunk, or Prem, or Reynolds are, my point was that the good-cop-bad-cop routine would not work on me because I am not your usual subject of an interrogation. You forget . . . I came to you! It should not be difficult to "crack" me, given that I am voluntarily giving you everything I possibly can. All you have to do is listen to it and believe it."

"Hey! Listening to and believing all of this shit is a lot tougher than any other interrogation I've ever done. But that's neither here nor there. Let's get back to this Kennedy business in the 1960s."

"Very well, but Mister Kennedy's awareness of the presence of my people on this planet predates his presidency by two decades."

"Come again."

"Mister Kennedy knew about aliens well before the 1960s. In fact, shortly after the July 1947 Roswell crash, MJ-12 created a document called "Interplanetary Phenomenon Unit Summary." Essentially, it was an overly wordy special group operations manual, and it laid out new policies pertaining to extraterrestrial entities—with special emphasis on recovering, using, and eventually disposing of alien technology."

"That was fourteen years before Kennedy became President," Abell pointed out.

"Yes, but I have read that manual, and it reveals the names of certain members of Congress who were given access to it after the Roswell incident. Several World War Two veterans were elected to Congress in 1946—among them John Kennedy, Richard Nixon, and Joseph McCarthy—and those men, due in large part to their recent military experience, were brought in as "consultants" after the Roswell incident. So, like Mister Nixon and Mister McCarthy, Mister Kennedy knew about our presence here as early as his freshman year in Congress. That is just one reason why Mister Kennedy was such an early and ardent supporter of NASA."

"You're saying that Kennedy wanted to go to the moon . . . ?"

"Because he knew that we were already there, using it as a staging area for our surveillance of your planet."

"Jesus! Who's going to tell Tom Hanks?" Abell muttered under his breath.

"I am not familiar with Tom Hanks. Was he an early founder of NASA, or was he with the LGBTQ agency?"

Abell did a classic spit take with a fair dose of Diet-Coke coming out through his nose. "Okay, I brought that one on myself. Forget Tom Hanks, but I can't imagine that your people were too thrilled about NASA and its progress."

"Indeed not. Even though their progress was painfully slow, it was still progress nonetheless, and we did everything we could to derail it."

"What about the three astronauts who died in a fire during a launch rehearsal for Apollo 1? Gus Grissom . . . Ed White and . . . ?"

"Roger Chaffee," Gabriel finished. "No. As I said before, some accidents are indeed just that, accidents. And that one wasn't us. However, it was no accident that, just one month after JFK's statement about putting a man on the moon by the end of the decade, the Cuban missile crisis began."

"That was you?" Abell asked skeptically.

"Yes. How else do you think you learned about the presence of Soviet-made nuclear missiles in Cuba?"

"It was from U2 spy flights over Cuba. Everybody knows that. Hell, they even . . ."

"Made a movie about it? Yes, I know. I, too, have seen *Thirteen Days*. Personally, I prefer *The Missiles of October*, but both movies render the accounts of the Cuban Missile Crisis no more faithfully than did *X-Men: First Class*."

"You're not claiming that your people were responsible for placing those missiles there in the first place?"

"No, of course not. However, the presence of the missiles presented much too valuable of an opportunity for us to simply sit back and hope for the best."

"The best being . . . ?"

"A nuclear war between the United States and the Soviet Union."

"Right."

"So we made certain that your Defense Department had ample evidence to support its proposed invasion of Cuba."

"And how did you do that?"

"Quite simply, we mailed the photographs to the Pentagon—much higher resolution ones, by the way, than could possibly have been taken by any man-made camera of the time."

"You mailed the pictures to the Pentagon?" Abell echoed incredulously.

"Sometimes the best solution is the easiest one. Unfortunately, it didn't work. Despite the hawkish stance taken by men like General Maxwell

Taylor, Former Secretary of State Dean Acheson, National Security Advisor McGeorge Bundy, and Air Force Chief of Staff Curtis "Bombs Away" LeMay, the Kennedy brothers found a way to avert a war. Fortunately for the survival of the human race, but unfortunately for us, those "wise old men" who were so hellbent on taking their new toys down off the shelf to play with were not listened to, and cooler heads prevailed. But it is no exaggeration to state that the world as you know it would not exist today but for the tactical brilliance of John Kennedy and the strategic foresight of his brother Robert."

"Yeah, I'm feeling really good about that one today myself."

"You should be. Had the Kennedy brothers listened to the "sage advice" of these hawks, as we hoped they would, your government would have invaded Cuba; the Soviets would have countered by invading West Berlin, and the missiles would have flown."

In a rare display of sincerity, Abell said, "I know. My father was in the 1st Infantry Division in 1962. The Big Red One. He was part of the 5th Howitzer battalion, 32nd artillery. And he was on a plane headed for Cuba when it all went down."

"He was to have been part of the invasion force?"

"Yep. He would have helped set up the headquarters for the field artillery. But on the day of the invasion, he would have had a different duty."

"What would that have been?" Gabriel asked, his curiosity genuine.

"His primary job would have been to jump on barbed wire so that other soldiers could step on his back and jump over the wire."

Gabriel looked exceedingly puzzled. "Why not just cut the wire?"

"Yeah—I don't know. I guess because we didn't have access to *alien knowhow* at the time."

"Actually, you did. Remember that the Roswell incident had occurred fifteen years earlier."

"Right. Well . . . there's a reason why they say that "military intelligence" is an oxymoron."

"Who are *they*?"

"Never mind. Let's get back to Kennedy. What happened next?"

"Well, after having cut a secret deal with Mr. Khrushchev to avert a war, Kennedy did everything he could to avoid being placed in that position again by the hawks in his military. He called for massive cuts to the defense budget, devised a plan to get all US personnel out of Vietnam by the end of 1965, created a plan for making the space race a cooperative venture with the Soviet Union, and signed a nuclear test ban treaty with Premier Khrushchev. Then, on November 8, 1963, just two weeks before his assassination, Kennedy issued a fateful . . . and fatal . . . decree. National Security Action Memorandum 271 ordered NASA administrator James Webb to initiate a joint space program with the Soviets. And just four days later he told CIA director John McCone that "unknowns in space" were posing a possible security threat to both the United States and the Soviet Union. Why do all of this? Well, in short, he was trying to end the Cold War—shelve any possibility of a Third World War so that the Americans and Soviets could marshal their considerable forces in a united effort against a common foe—us."

Gabriel paused in reflection for a moment before continuing. "In hindsight, it appeared that we might have . . . *backed the wrong horse*, as you say. Perhaps we would have been better off allowing Nixon to win the 1960 presidential election. After all, had he been president in October of 1962, nuclear war would almost certainly have been waged."

"I never really thought about it that way," Abell admitted.

Gabriel smiled. "Of course not. You can afford to be that shortsighted. We couldn't. And realizing our mistake, we had to correct it."

Abell let that statement hang in the air for a moment before responding. "You . . . *corrected* it?"

"Yes. If we wanted to increase the chances of your two countries going to war, then we needed someone like Leonid Brezhnev to replace Nikita Khrushchev, and . . ."

"And . . . ?"

"We needed to put a Texan in the White House. That's why we could no longer afford to let John Kennedy live."

CHAPTER SEVENTEEN

"I just knew that we were going to end up here," Abell confessed. "I just knew that I wasn't getting out of here today without you confessing to the Kennedy assassination. Did you also kidnap the Lindbergh baby? Do you know where Jimmy Hoffa's body is buried?"

"No. I'm afraid I can't help you there, Agent Adamson. I believe that Bruno Hauptmann was already falsely convicted of and executed for the kidnapping of Charles A. Lindbergh, Jr. And I doubt that Mr. Hoffa's remains will ever be found. Besides which, neither Mister Lindbergh nor Mister Hoffa ever posed any sort of threat to my people. However, because he was attempting to significantly deescalate East-West tensions, Mister Kennedy did pose such a threat. Would you like to know how it was done?"

"How what was done?" Cane asked as he reentered the room.

"The Kennedy assassination. I was just about to come get you," Abell lied.

"Hell yeah, we'd like to know how it was done! Abell, think of how much of a jump in paygrade we will both get when we come into the boss's office with the truth about the Kennedy . . ."

"You may find this amusing, Agent Canyon. But I assure you, I do not. My people did not take this action lightly. But we had no choice but to eliminate Mister Kennedy, and to do so in a way that left scant or contradictory evidence."

"You had no choice?" Cane echoed. "What did JFK ever do to you? Let me guess, he was sleeping with some of the top aliens' wives, right? Playing a little pickle tickle with the girls from Mars? Maybe messing around on *Your Anus*?"

Abell turned towards his partner with a look that was part bemusement and part wonder.

"What's gotten into you? Where did you go for a break . . . the strip club?"

Cane smiled. "Nope, but I did just get a steamy voicemail from Sasha . . . and some great new pictures, too. Want to see them?"

"Absolutely not!" Abell protested. "I'm going to have a hard enough time falling asleep tonight without having to add your adventures in sexting to the list of stuff rattling around in my brain. Besides, did you know that Bruno Hauptmann was falsely convicted of kidnapping the Lindbergh baby?"

"Is that a fact?"

"Yep. And I'll fill you in later as to *why* our friends from outer space had to ice Kennedy. For now, I just want to hear *how* they did it." He then turned his attention back towards Gabriel and asked, "Was Oswald one of you?"

Gabriel laughed. "Oswald? You can't be serious. Lee Harvey Oswald had about as much to do with the Kennedy assassination as Bruno Hauptmann did. In fact, Mister Oswald was exactly what he claimed to be—a patsy. He was simply in the wrong place at the wrong time . . . or the right place at the right time, depending on one's perspective. At the time of the assassination, Oswald was in a break room on the second floor of the Texas School Book Depository building drinking a Coke. In fact, he was credibly placed there by at least three different witnesses, including his own boss and a Dallas police officer named Marion Baker. However, Oswald's rather sordid past had brought him into contact with unsavory figures in both the intelligence community and the world of organized crime. Therefore, when the Dallas Police Department and the Texas Rangers and the Secret Service and the FBI were all trying to figure out what had happened . . . or at least trying to make it look like they were trying to figure out what happened . . . well, he was just too good of a catch to release back in the water."

"So, how *did* you do it?" Cane asked. "Was it one shooter or two? Three bullets or four?"

"I hate to disappoint you both, but there were no shooters at all. And there was actually no bullet at all, not in the technical sense of the term. All other "evidence," including the 6.5mm Model 91/38 Mannlicher-Carcano bolt-action rifle and the three cartridges found on the sixth floor of the Texas school book depository building, was placed in and around Dealey Plaza to make the investigation extremely difficult. As it turns out, however, we needn't have been so diligent. The people your government appointed to investigate the murder had about as much desire to solve the case as . . ."

"What?"

"I'm sorry. I'm just unable to come up with a metaphor that would aptly describe just how inept the Warren Commission's investigation truly was. There simply aren't words in the English language to properly express their level of incompetence."

"You can say that again," Cane agreed. As something of a Kennedy assassination aficionado, Cane had read virtually every book (of which there were hundreds) ever written on the subject, and he was convinced that Oswald had not acted alone, and that the Warren Commission had not acted in good faith.

"Okay," Abell interrupted. "Let's not go too far down that rabbit hole. Just cut to the chase. How did you do it?"

"We used a very simple electromagnetic propulsion device."

"Come again?" Cane asked as Abell wrote something in his notes.

"Electromagnetic propulsion is a practical application of science in which one accelerates an object by the utilization of a flowing electrical current and magnetic fields. We've been using it for centuries, but you first became aware of it in the late nineteenth century. Look up the work of the English-born Professor Elihu Thomson. It was quite groundbreaking research, at least for a human, anyway. It is now commonly used in transportation systems, like maglev railcars, to minimize friction and maximize speed over long distances. It is also frequently utilized in your theme parks to create high-speed roller coasters and water rides."

"But you used it to kill Kennedy?"

"Yes. As Kennedy's motorcade passed by the crowd in Dealey Plaza, one of our people held a simple projectile in his hand. It wasn't a "bullet" per se, but its shape and density would come the closest to being one of your 5.56x45mm rimless bottlenecked rounds, and it most definitely did not match the caliber of the rifle we planted in the sixth-floor window of the warehouse. Another one of us used a simple electromagnetic device to propel that one "bullet" back and forth through the motorcade multiple times, inflicting three wounds to the president—one through the front of the throat, one in the upper back, and the fatal blow to the head. Unfortunately, the operator of the device got carried away and struck Governor Connally several times, as well as an innocent bystander. This accounts for all of the discrepancies between the number of the wounds, the direction from which they came, and the angles at which they entered the victim's bodies."

"Okay, first of all, there was no wounded innocent bystander," Abell pointed out.

"Yes there was," Cane corrected. "James Tague."

"Who?"

"James Thomas Tague. He was a Dallas car salesman who suffered a minor wound to his right cheek as he was standing by the triple underpass watching the motorcade. It was caused by tiny fragments of concrete—debris that flew up when a bullet . . . or some other *projectile* . . . struck the curb near where he was standing."

Gabriel smiled. "Quite right."

"Fine—but no *5.56x45mm rimless bottlenecked round* was found anywhere near Dealey Plaza that day. In fact, I don't think a round like that even existed in 1963."

"No, of course not. To further confuse the investigation, which we had erroneously believed would have been conducted in good faith, we used a projectile that did not match the caliber of any bullet in production anywhere in the world at that time. And the reason the projectile was never recovered is because it was ultimately returned to the hand of the person . . . *alien* . . . who released it in the first place."

"*AND* . . ." Abell continued, not at all disheartened by Gabriel's incorrigible ability to answer all of his questions, ". . . there's no way a person . . . alien or otherwise . . . could have operated an . . ."

"Electromagnetic propulsion device," Gabriel offered helpfully.

"Right! There's no way anyone could operate an alien ray gun right out in the middle of all of those people—including Dallas police officers, network reporters, Secret Service agents, and only God knows how many spectators—without being seen."

"You're absolutely right, Agent Adamson. That's why we had to disguise the device."

"As what?" Abell asked, fuming.

"As an umbrella," Cane answered before Gabriel could.

"As an umbrella," Gabriel confirmed, nodding. "Quite right."

*****

Still skeptical, Abell asked, "Why not just put the device in Abraham Zapruder's video camera? He had a perfect position, and no one would have thought twice about seeing someone moving a camera around."

"Because Abraham Zapruder wasn't one of us. We had no idea who he was, nor that he would be there, nor that he would have a camera. The "umbrella man," however, *was* one of us, and we were able to disguise his device in plain sight."

Despite finding some truth to Gabriel's outlandish claims, Cane decided to play the role of devil's advocate. "But the "umbrella man," as you called him, was identified. In fact, he outed himself to the United States House Select Committee on Assassinations in 1978. His name was Louie Steven Witt, and he voluntarily came forward to admit to Congressional investigators that he brought the signature black umbrella that day to heckle Kennedy. It was to be a subtle but sarcastic reference to Joseph P. Kennedy's support of Neville Chamberlain and his policies of appeasing Hitler in the 1930s."

"Quite right, Agent Canyon. But I can assure you that my people have absolutely no idea who Louie Steven Witt is, nor what his motivations were for making such false claims. Perhaps he simply wanted his fifteen minutes of fame. But the . . . *person* . . . who carried that umbrella was actually named *Açətirchhati-mazla*, at least that's how his name would be pronounced in your language. And if you watch the films and photographs of the assassination carefully, you will see that he was one of the closest bystanders to the motorcade when the President was first struck, and you will further notice that he opened the umbrella, spun it around clockwise—from east to west—as the president's motorcade passed him by. You will also notice that another man, a dark complected *person* who was never identified, was sitting on the sidewalk next to *Açǝtirchhati-mazla*. Both men remained perfectly calm throughout the entire event and were the only two in Dealey Plaza who did not react in any way to the "shots." Then, as everyone else was still diving for cover or running around hysterically, they calmly stood up and went their separate ways."

"I remember him, too," Cane said. "I think the Warren Commission simply called him "Dark Complected Man," because they could never identify him."

"That's right. His actual name, at least as you would pronounce it, was *Temnýranliq-qorong'u*, and he was the one who released and then retrieved the "bullet" that was used to kill Kennedy and wound Governor Connally and James Tague."

"It was bright and sunny in Dallas that day," Abell reminded Gabriel. "Weren't any of your *people* at all concerned with the fact that a man opening and closing an umbrella would draw a great deal of attention to himself?"

"Yes, but the forecast had been for rain that day. That's why we chose to place the device in the umbrella in the first place. In fact, when the President was in Fort Worth earlier that morning, it had been raining. So, it didn't seem out of place for *Açǝtirchhati-mazla* to have an umbrella on him. And as far as his maneuvering it around, everyone was too shocked and too focused on the reality of the drama playing out in front of them to notice something as mundane as that. It was quite ingenious, I assure you. And it achieved the desired result. With Kennedy dead and Lyndon B. Johnson in the White House, the spirit of cooperation with the Communists that Kennedy had engendered was quickly erased. But, just to be sure, we had Nikita Khrushchev replaced by Leonid Brezhnev the following year. But how we did that is a tale for another time."

"We're going to assume for a second that everything you just said is true," Cane began.

"We're going to do what?!" Abell cried.

"Just play along with me for a minute," he said curtly to his partner. Then, turning his attention back to Gabriel, said, "Assuming all of that is true, why then kill Oswald? If he was just a patsy, and if the two real assassins . . . whatever their names were . . . just walked away, why kill

Oswald? If he truly was an uninvolved, innocent bystander, then there would have been no need to silence him."

"We didn't."

"I beg your pardon."

"We didn't 'silence' him. We didn't know anything about Jack Ruby. Apparently, he was just a deranged pimp and a strip club owner. He was a nobody. It worked out beautifully when he murdered Oswald on live television, however, as it brought all sorts of new conspiracy elements to the whole affair. And those various conspiracies, not one of them anywhere close to the truth, have kept you all spinning ever since. Here you are, sixty years later, and you're still trying to figure out who shot from what window."

Cane and Abell spent several long seconds quietly staring at Gabriel.

He silently stared back.

Only when Gabriel took a sip from his water bottle did Cane break the awkward silence.

"What's your name?" he asked.

"I'm sorry."

"Earlier, you said we would not be able to pronounce your name. But you just told us how we would pronounce the names of the two assassins . . ."

"And you also told me earlier that the name of your planet is *Ev jiāllar-ɵŭ*," Abell reminded Gabriel.

Fluent in four different languages (English, Polish, German, and Russian), Cane was impressed with Abell's ability to pronounce the unpronounceable. But he showed no reaction other than to continue to stare at Gabriel. "So, what's your name? How would we say it?"

"*Аɸəрешmənxə-ıɸlyrba*."

Another long and awkward silence ensued.

"Then what?" Cane eventually said, trying to resume the interrogation. "Kennedy was dead. Johnson and Brezhnev were in office. Then what?"

"Nothing."

"Nothing?" Abell repeated.

"Nothing. At least not until 1973."

"Why the ten-year hiatus?" Cane wanted to know.

"In short—the Vietnam War. Between you, the Soviets, the Chinese, and the Vietnamese—to say nothing of what was going on in the Middle East between 1963 and 1973—we thought, once again, that you humans had a better chance of killing yourselves than reaching the stars to harm us. We really thought . . . and hoped . . . that you would save us the trouble of doing it ourselves."

"And then . . . ?"

"And then, by the end of October of 1973, the Yom Kippur War had ended, the Samita border skirmish between Kuwait and Iraq had quieted down, and American involvement in Vietnam was coming to an end. And Mister Nixon was fully embroiled in the Watergate scandal, leaving us to wonder who the next "leader of the free world" would be. At that time, we understood nothing about the procedures for presidential succession under the terms of your Constitution. Eventually, however, after a ten-year lull in our activities, we had to . . . resume our intervention."

"And where did you start that time?" Abell asked. "With Gerald Ford?"

"No, in a rather unlikely place. With Jackie Gleason."

CHAPTER EIGHTEEN

"Jackie Gleason? The comedian?" Cane asked in surprise.

"Please don't tell me that Jackie Gleason was really an alien named something like *Глейсон-ипиһйă*," Abell said.

Gabirel stared knowingly back at Abell, while Cane again marveled at his partner's ability to pronounce the unpronounceable. "No, Agent Adamson. Mister Gleason was not an alien. He was, however, a close personal friend of Richard Nixon's, and at some point in 1973, I'm still not entirely sure when, Nixon revealed a series of alien secrets to Mister Gleason, even going so far as to take him to Homestead Air Force Base in Florida so that he could see some of the bodies for himself. Since the bodies were small, only about two feet tall and with disproportionately large heads, Gleason initially thought the bodies belonged to deformed children."

"Small and with disproportionately large heads? He could be talking about you, Abell." Cane joked.

Ignoring the good-natured jab, Abell knitted his brow and stared hard at Gabriel. "Well, you're not two feet tall; and your head is proportional to the rest of your body; and you're not a muted gray like you said earlier. Are you sure you're an alien?"

"I'm quite certain, Agent. When we are . . . *undercover* . . . we have to assume the physical characteristics of those around us."

"*Kiedy wszedłeś między wrony, musisz krakać jak i one,*" Cane said.

"What does that one mean?" Abell asked.

"The literal translation is, *When you have stepped among the crows, you must caw as well.* It's the Polish equivalent to, *When in Rome . . .*'"

"You still don't believe me, do you?" Gabriel asked.

Neither Cane nor Abell said a word.

"Maybe I could borrow that paperclip?" Gabriel asked Cane.

A confused look on his face, Cane slipped a paperclip off of the set of files in front of him and handed it to Gabriel, who quickly straightened it out. Then, dragging one of the exposed ends painfully down the entire length of his left arm, he set it aside. As a tiny line of blood beaded up along the shallow wound he had scratched into his arm, Gabriel saw the look of disbelief on the faces of both agents.

"It's blue," they both said at the same time.

All Gabriel offered by way of a response was, "So, I guess we're done talking about Richard Nixon and Jackie Gleason."

*****

Standing outside the interrogation room, Cane and Abell just stared at each other.

"What the fuck was that?" Cane finally whispered, careful not to draw any attention from the other agents in the office.

"I don't know," Abell admitted. "But it has to be some kind of parlor trick. I heard somewhere once that human blood is actually blue until it becomes oxygenated. That if it existed in a vacuum, without air, it would be blue. Maybe he . . ."

"Found a way to separate the oxygen from his blood?" Cane asked skeptically. "Doubtful. And I've heard that about human blood, too. It turns out it's just an urban legend. Our blood is always red because it contains a large number of red blood cells, which contain hemoglobin."

"So how did he pull off that little trick?" Abell wondered aloud.

"I don't know, but there's something I want to check out before we go back in there."

"Fine, but I'm about to cut him loose. I can't see where he has committed any crime, and I'm beginning to wonder if someone at CPD is just jerking our chains a little. Who was that captain down there who was pulling all of the practical jokes on his people all of the time?"

"Sutkamp," Cane reminded him.

"Right, Sutkamp. Remember when he brought in a cake for his squad that he said his wife had baked for them? Turns out it was made of soap."

"Maybe. But while Sutkamp might screw around with his own guys, I don't see him trying to pull off something this elaborate. That guy in there is the real deal. I don't mean that he is an alien, but he sure as hell thinks he's one. Maybe we should get one of the Psych boys to take a look at him."

"Okay. I'll put in a call to Doctor Strangelove. Let's see what he thinks."

*****

Doctor Stephen Strenlowe was a tall and thin man with bright red hair, a long and sharp nose, and piercing green eyes that remained partially obscured by an expensive and hopelessly out of date pair of pince-nez glasses. Undeniably brilliant in the fields of both criminal and forensic psychology, he was also what his co-workers liked to call *peculiar*. For example, he often joked that his very full head of bright red hair, which made him look a little like Ronald McDonald, was the result of his mother having been on her period when his father had gotten her pregnant. In fact, despite being extremely well-respected by his fellow agents, he was so eccentric that they commonly referred to him as *Doctor Strangelove*—an homage to Peter Sellers' eponymous character from Stanley Kubrick's iconic 1964 political satire film.

Called in by Agents Canyon and Adamson, he spent several hours that afternoon with Gabriel while Abell and Cane tried to figure out how their "suspect" had pulled off the trick with the blue blood.

When he finally emerged from the sweatbox with pages of notes he had taken, he smiled at the awaiting Cane and Abell.

"What do you think?"

"I don't think he's crazy, if that's what you're asking. But I do think he's the best actor this side of Daniel Day Lewis. Talk about method acting. He is beyond committed to the role; he genuinely thinks he is a visitor from another planet."

"Did he tell you about Jackie Gleason?"

Strenlowe referred to some of his notes before continuing. "No, but did you know that the reason the Apollo moon-landing program was abandoned was because NASA had no way to protect its astronauts from the aliens who were already up there? Apparently, the little green men . . . I'm sorry, little *gray* men . . . had established a base of operations on the moon, and we could no longer protect our guys. Oh, by the way, the whole reason for the space program in the first place wasn't to beat the Soviets into space. It was all part of something called *Project Horizon*—a plan to establish a base on the moon to strike at them before they entered Earth's atmosphere."

"That's nuts!" Abell asserted.

"No, it's not. Shockingly, it is actually quite true," Strenlowe assured him. "I looked it up while I was in there with him. In 1959, back when primary responsibility for our space program was in the hands of the military, they put together a study to determine whether or not it was feasible to construct a military base on the moon. In fact, in June of '59, a group at the Army Ballistic Missile Agency issued a report entitled . . ." Strenlowe paused to consult his notes before continuing. *"A United States Army Study for the Establishment of a Lunar Military Outpost.* They made a budget request and everything. It was supposed to be operational and manned by twelve soldiers or sailors or airmen as early as December 1966."

"What happened?" Cane asked.

"It never progressed past the feasibility stage because primary responsibility for our space program was transferred to NASA—a civilian agency."

"How does he know all of this stuff?" Abell asked.

"I told you, he has really committed to his role. He has obviously studied—a lot! For example, did you know that the reason the United States and the Soviet Union had ten times the number of nuclear warheads needed to completely destroy the entire planet had nothing to do with a nuclear deterrent? That stockpile wasn't to destroy the planet, it was to save it." He consulted his notes again before adding, "If the men from outer space invaded and obliterated either one of the two superpowers, then the other one would still have sufficient fire power to retaliate."

"And if the Klingons . . . or whatever they are . . . destroyed both superpowers?" Cane wondered.

"I asked him that. He said that the US and the USSR had a secret joint agreement dating back to the Kennedy years that, if both were overrun, they would fire all of their missiles at each other."

"Why?"

Strenlowe read from his notes and said, "To . . . 'render the planet inhospitable for habitation by any living creature.' A sort of *the bad guys won the battle but lost the war* kind of thing, I guess. I'm telling you, that guy has an answer for everything. We stopped when we got into the Reagan years because he began to wonder when, or if, you two were planning on coming back in. I guess he misses you two. Oh—and he wants more water and pretzels, by the way. And he has a nasty scratch on one arm. I hope for your sake that neither one of you did that to him."

Neither Cane nor Abell wanted to mention anything about Gabriel's trick with the blue blood to Strenlowe, but Cane did have one more question for him. "Well, what do you think, Doc? You spent most of the afternoon with him. What's your professional opinion?"

Strenlowe closed up his notes and took off his glasses. "My professional opinion is that he's perfectly sane, utterly brilliant, and staging a performance for the ages. I'm serious, he should get an Oscar, an Emmy, and a Tony for this. My advice is to send him back down to CPD and forget all about it, because I don't think he's going to ever run out of material. He has obviously been preparing for this performance for a really long time."

"Why would someone do that?" Abell wondered aloud.

"*Nie mój cyrk, nie moje małpy,*" Strenlowe said, repeating a phrase he had often heard Cane utter. Literally translated, it meant, *Not my circus, not my monkeys.* Essentially, it was a polite Polish way of saying, *Not my problem.*

"I'm sorry to simply leave it at that, but . . ."

"But you're going to, aren't you?" Cane asked, impressed with Strenlowe's nearly perfect pronunciation of the Polish idiom.

"Look, it's almost five o'clock already and my daughter has a soccer game tonight that I do not want to miss. So, I bid you *adieu*, gentlemen. Thank you for providing me with a very interesting and amusing afternoon."

"And what are we supposed to do with Flash Gordon in there?" Abell asked.

"That's for you two to figure out. That's why you guys get paid the big bucks."

"And why we get all of the girls, too, huh?" Abell added.

"Well, for Cowboy anyway," Strenlowe joked. With that, he headed back to his office on the third floor, leaving Cane and Abell to stare at a floor of the building that was rapidly emptying of agents and other employees.

"*Just another manic Monday*," Cane sang to himself again.

CHAPTER NINETEEN

The two agents waited another hour before going back in, sometime around 6:00 pm, as the office began to quiet down for the day. They also decided to try to take a different approach with Gabriel—a more passive-aggressive one.

As they reentered the room, Cane said to Abell, "Did you know that human blood is red because it contains hemoglobin, which is a red-colored, iron-containing protein?"

"You don't say?" Abell responded, playing his part to a tee.

"I do say. Did you also know that, contrary to a popular misconception, human blood does not appear blue under any circumstances? However, there are some animals that do have blue blood."

"I didn't know that either. What kinds of animals?"

"Well, I'm glad you asked that, Abell. It seems that spiders, mollusks, and certain arthropods use hemocyanin in their hemolymph, which is similar to our blood, but that copper-based pigment is blue."

"How about that?" Abell said, feigning interest.

Gabriel, seemingly amused, smiled and said, "That was quite a little performance the two of you just put on. Please don't tell me that you spent all afternoon writing and rehearsing that dialogue. And, while you both seem to be knowledgeable about a great many things, I highly doubt that either of you knows the first thing about hemocyanin, hemolymph, or arthropods."

"Oh, we weren't performing," Abell assured Gabriel. "We just wanted you to know that we already knew how easy it would be to fake that blue blood trick."

Gabriel's smile widened and he nodded his head. "Perhaps. But I do seem to be fresh out of spiders and mollusks at the moment, so that would make it difficult for me to render just such an illusion."

Already bored with the science fair drama they had been playing out, Cane said, "Fine, let's switch from zoology to psychiatry. Where do you leave off with Doctor Strenlowe?"

"Well, I believe we were just about to talk about the failed assassination attempt against Ronald Reagan in 1981, but then he left. Something about a young girls' soccer game."

"You tried to kill Reagan?" Abell asked. "John Hinkley, Jr. was . . . *one of yours?*"

"Yes and no. We did try to kill Reagan, but John Hinckley, Jr. was not . . . *one of ours.* He was simply a deranged human obsessed with some actress by the name of Jodie Foster. One of . . . *us* . . . stumbled upon him, quite by accident, and expertly used his bizarre obsession for our own purposes."

"Which were what? What purpose could have been served by killing Ronald Reagan?"

"We tried to eliminate Mister Reagan in 1981 because of the massive arms buildup he was planning, and because of his so-called Strategic Defense Initiative. He wasn't ready to reveal all of his plans just yet, but we had learned about them in late 1979 or early 1980, around the same time the public was becoming aware of your Space Shuttle program. Both were really part of a covert cold war against aliens."

"But the assassination attempt against Reagan was in 1981, and he didn't announce SDI until 1983."

"Yes, but he had begun to think about it as early as 1979, even before he was elected. The concept of a missile defense system intended to protect the United States from attack by ballistic nuclear weapons, whether they were intercontinental ballistic missiles or submarine-launched ballistic missiles, was announced on March 23, 1983, and it was quickly and derisively nicknamed the "*Star Wars* program" by its detractors. But development of such a program had begun in the mid-1970s, and it began in the Soviet Union, not the United States."

"The Soviets were experimenting with SDI in the 1970s?" Abell asked incredulously.

"Of course. From where do you suppose your President Reagan got the idea? Terrified by the concept of Mutually Assured Destruction, the Soviets began experimenting with a laser-based orbital weapons platform, as well as an anti-satellite low-orbit missile platform."

"How come we never heard of that before?" Cane asked.

"They don't call it Top Secret without reason, Agent Canyon. The Soviets are not usually eager to share their most trusted secrets with American civilians and/or agents of the FBI. You didn't hear about it because they didn't want you to."

"The Soviets?"

"Yes, as well as your own government. In 1979, Presidential candidate Ronald Reagan visited the NORAD command base at Cheyenne Mountain, where he was first introduced to the extensive tracking and detection systems already extending throughout the world and into space; however, he was struck by the fact that, while NORAD could *track* an incoming missile attack down to the individual targets, there was nothing they could do to actually *stop* one. Reagan felt that, in the event of an attack, the president would be placed in a terrible position, having to choose between immediate counterattack or attempting to absorb the attack and then maintain an upper hand in the post-attack era. This feeling of helplessness, coupled with the innovative ideas proposed by the Soviets, which your government's spies had just learned about, combined to form the impetus for SDI. However, as the Soviets soon learned, the science just wasn't there yet. The Soviets continued to push forward, but your government decided to move in another direction."

"The Space Shuttle program?"

"Yes—that and the International Space Station program. Both had already proceeded past the conceptual stage by the late 1960s. The Shuttle program formally commenced in 1972 and, after the Apollo and Skylab programs of the 1970s, became the sole focus of NASA's human spaceflight operations. Originally conceived of and presented to the public in 1972 as a sort-of . . . *space truck*, I guess . . . the Shuttles would, among other things, be used to help build the low-Earth-orbit International Space Station. Both programs received additional focus and funding after Reagan's 1979 trip to Cheyenne Mountain, but while the Space Shuttle program was phenomenally successful, the ISS program suffered from long delays, design changes, and major cost overruns. Ultimately, however, the advances made in both programs eventually fueled further SDI research."

"Speaking of the Space Shuttles, did you blow up either one of them?" Cane asked.

"No. As I told you before, neither the *Challenger* disaster in 1986 nor the *Columbia* accident in 2003 were our fault. Both were the results of your own incompetence . . . or negligence."

Abell summarized: "So as early as 1981, you knew of Reagan's plan to launch SDI. And you were threatened by that, so you made the decision to kill him. But if you had successfully killed Reagan, George H. W. Bush would have been president."

"Yes, we now understood your presidential succession, even if your own people did not, and President Bush would have been an even greater threat to us than President Reagan."

"So why go through it?" Cane asked.

"Well, we planned to kill George Bush later that same day."

Cane turned towards Abell. "Who was Speaker of the House in 1981?"

"Tip O'Neill."

"That's correct, and . . ."

But Cane cut him off. "Wait—a second ago you said that you understood our presidential succession even though we did not. What did you mean by that?"

"When Reagan was shot in 1981, there was some great confusion about the constitutional order of succession. In response to a question about who was in charge while the President was under anesthesia and Vice-president Bush was travelling abroad, your Secretary of State Alexander Haig famously, or infamously, said that *he* was in control; in reality, however, he was fourth in line after Vice-president Bush, Speaker of the House O'Neill, and President pro Tempore of the Senate Strom Thurmond—and what a nightmare for you and victory for us that would have been."

"So how were you planning on taking Bush out after you killed Reagan?"

"Mister Bush was 1,300 miles away and 30,000 feet up. Ironically, he had just unveiled a plaque at the Hotel Texas in Fort Worth where President Kennedy had spent his last night alive. He had then boarded Air Force Two for a short flight from Fort Worth to Austin, Texas, where he was to deliver a speech to the Texas legislature. We fired an EMP burst from one of our aircraft at his plane, but we failed to crash it. Apparently, Air Force Two, like its sister ship, has a series of redundant electronic systems. The EMP burst did, however, cripple the plane's secure voice communications system, which meant that Bush could not communicate with officials in Washington, which is what led to the Secretary of State's unfortunate blunder."

"So, and I can't believe I'm about to say this," Cane confessed, "but had you killed both Reagan and Bush, your people would not have felt threatened by a President Tip O'Neill?"

"No, we would not. While his Republican detractors had mislabeled him as just another "tax-and-spend, bleeding-heart liberal," he was far from it. In fact, while not exactly a hawk, he had supported Democratic Congressman Charlie Wilson's efforts to work with Gust Avrakotos of the CIA to steer billions of dollars to the Mujahideen who were fighting the Soviets in Afghanistan. I believe they even made a movie about it, Agent Canyon. So, he was not your typical liberal."

"Then why would he have been an improvement over Reagan . . . or Bush?" Abell asked.

"Because he was no fan of Reagan's excessive arms buildup or his SDI initiative. While O'Neill was right that SDI was too expensive, too risky, and too pie-in-the-sky . . . that was only true for the moment. Had it proceeded, the Soviets would have attempted to match or exceed it, meaning that it would have become the next logical step in mankind's militarization of the heavens. Additionally, Reagan—who was essentially a puppet of George Bush, much in the same way that Bush's son was later a puppet of Vice-president Dick Cheney—was well aware of our presence and the threat we posed to your people. Tip O'Neill, however, who naively thought the biggest threat posed to the world was the presence of Communists in Afghanistan, was not."

"Reagan was . . . *aware* . . . of you?" Cane asked.

"Yes. While his acting abilities were mid-level at best, his talents at keeping secrets were honed. It was not until his Alzheimer's disease began to worsen that he revealed his true thinking. In September of 1987, an aging and declining Mister Reagan gave a remarkable speech to the United Nations General Assembly. In an often-quoted section of that speech, Reagan asked a series of shocking rhetorical questions and commented about the nations and cultures of the world uniting in common efforts to live in peace and avoid wars and bloodshed."

Rather than leave the room, Cane simply got out his phone, looked up the text of the speech and began to read portions of it aloud. "Here it is: Reagan said, *'Cannot swords be turned to plowshares? Can we and all nations not live in peace? In our obsession with antagonisms of the moment, we often forget how much unites all the members of humanity.'*

"He goes on to say, *'Perhaps we need some outside, universal threat to make us recognize this common bond.'* Whoa!"

Abell groaned and rolled his eyes, prompting his partner to continue. "Listen to this, Abell: *I occasionally think how quickly our differences worldwide would vanish if we were facing an alien threat from outside this world. And yet, I ask you, is not an alien force already among us? What could be more alien to the universal aspirations of our peoples than war and the threat of war?'* What do you think about that?"

"I think he was talking about the threat of nuclear war!" Abell practically shouted.

"Was he?" Gabriel countered. "You think that the threat of nuclear war constituted an *'outside, universal threat'* in 1987? You really think that President Reagan would have described the threat of nuclear war as an *'alien force already among us?'* I hardly think so, Agent Adamson; nor did President Reagan. In this speech, the truth of which could only be revealed by his declining mental faculties, Reagan is clearly suggesting that the diverse cultures and societies all over your planet should set aside their differences and keep in mind the larger threat to all human culture. He was talking about us—the threat posed to *your* people by *mine*! And virtually every one of your most prominent leaders since then has understood the same. Why do you suppose former House Speaker Newt Gingrich proposed colonizing the moon in 2016? Or why former President Trump, unhinged as he was . . . is . . . announced the creation of a *Space Force*?"

"Because like most Republicans, they're both batshit crazy," Cane answered quickly as he continued to scan the text of Reagan's speech on his phone.

At the same time, Abell—as he had been doing all day—continued to scrutinize Gabriel's face, looking for the slightest hint that he was lying. Trained to recognize these micro-expressions which often belied a person's true intent, Abell had not found one until just then. Then, having seen it, he quickly made an excuse to leave the room.

"I . . . uh . . . have to go make a phone call," he offered lamely as Cane nodded and remained fully engrossed in his phone.

After Abell left, Gabriel exhaled loudly and seemed to deflate. Then he said, "He doesn't have to make a phone call."

But Cane never heard him. Nor, due to the soundproof nature of the interrogation room, did either Cane or Gabriel hear the seven shots that rang out in the outer office, all fired from Abell's standard-issue SIG Sauer P226 9mm pistol.

CHAPTER TWENTY

As the two men awaited Abell's return, Cane read something from his phone. "How about this? This is an official statement from the Obama White House: *'The US government has no evidence that any life exists outside our planet, or that an extraterrestrial presence has contacted any member of the human race . . . In addition, there is no credible information to suggest that any evidence is being hidden from the public's eye.'* See—not all of our leaders are looney tunes like Nixon, Reagan, Gingrich, and Trump."

"Have you already forgotten your Bismarck, Agent Canyon? *'Never believe anything in politics until it has been officially denied.'* That statement by your President Obama clearly . . ."

Just then, a somewhat disheveled Abell reentered, interrupting Gabriel's pronouncement.

"What's up? Who did you have to call?" Cane asked.

"He didn't have to call anyone," Gabriel answered for Abell, reading something on the agent's face that had not been there before. "Unless I miss my mark, Agent Adamson left to ensure that the video and audio recording devices in this room were turned off, and that any record that had been made so far had been erased. Isn't that right, Agent Adamson?"

Abell just smiled as Cane noticed a hint of a blood spatter on his partner's shirt.

"Abell, what's he talking about? And who did you just go call?"

Answering again for the agent, Gabriel added, "I imagine that he also checked to see if everyone else had left the office for the day; and, if they hadn't, he killed them."

"I wasn't asking you!" Cane shouted at Gabriel, incensed. "Abell, what is he talking about? What the hell is going on here? And who did you just call?"

"You were warned and warned and warned," Abell finally said to Gabriel, with an almost tsk-tsk quality to his voice. Then, shaking his head disapprovingly, he added, "But you just couldn't help yourself, could you?"

"What caused you to finally believe me?" Gabriel asked.

"Your eyes. Just before I left, I noticed the film that closed vertically across your eyes when you blinked. I hadn't noticed that before."

"Ah," Gabriel responded, making an exaggerated show of blinking so that Cane, too, could see the opaque film that closed, like a pair of sliding doors, across his eyes when he blinked. "In your case, Agent Adamson, it was your remarkable ability to pronounce words that no human should be able to. It didn't dawn on me until just a few minutes ago."

"What are you two talking about? What's going on here, Abell? And who did you call?"

"Gabriel has been telling the truth all along, cowboy. Since at least 1947, aliens have, in fact, been the architects of world politics and economics. But now, we're planning to do more than just meddle. We're no longer going to be quite so passive. Thanks, in part, to Trump's Space Force announcement, and the fact Russia, India, and the European Space Agency are all planning to launch missions to the Moon and even further into deep space this year, we have decided that now is the time to act, and we mean to . . . *eliminate the threat* . . . posed by humans—all humans, regardless of nationality. But *Aφəреишмənхə-ιφlуrbа* here just couldn't keep his mouth shut. His conscience wouldn't allow him to remain silent, and he just had to come forward to try to sound the alarm to someone. So, I had to contact my superiors on *Ev jiāllar-өŭ* to find out how they wanted the problem solved."

"I have grown quite fond of the people on this planet, Agent Adamson— or whatever your real name is. Because of that fondness, I simply wanted them to be ready when it happens—which I imagine will now be very soon. Like Prometheus, who gave the gift of fire to your people, marking the beginning of human innovation and technology, I had hoped to give humans the gift of some foresight, so that they could avoid what is to come."

"Well, you failed. And you know I can't let you leave here alive now," Abell said, ominously placing his right hand at his hip.

"What the fuck is going on here, Abell?" Cane demanded. "I'm getting really confused and extremely pissed off!"

Gabriel then proceeded to say something in a series of clicks and sounds that Cane could not identify.

"What did you just say?" Cane asked, aware that Abell now had his hand on his Bureau issued SIG Sauer 9mm pistol.

Sighing heavily, Abell said, "He just quoted from a letter written by Sir Thomas More to his daughter, Mistress Margaret Roper, in May of 1535. It said, *'I do none harm. I say none harm. I think none harm. And if this be not enough to keep a man alive, in good faith I long not to live.'* Isn't that right, *Аɸəpeɯɯənxə-ıɸlyrba*?"

"How do you know that?" Cane shouted, reaching for his own weapon.

Ignoring his partner's pleas for an explanation, Abell drew his weapon and said, "Very well, *Gabriel*. If you long not to live, I can accommodate that for you." He then proceeded to open fire, placing one round into Gabriel's head and several rounds into his chest.

Inside the confined space of the soundproofed room, the three shots sounded like canon fire, and as brain tissue and bright blue blood sprayed all over the room, Gabriel slumped backwards into his chair. At the same time, Cane jumped out of his, drawing his weapon and aiming it at his partner.

"What the fuck, Abell?! What did you just do?"

"We tried to warn him," Abell assured Cane. "No one on *Ev jiāllar-ɵŭ* wanted him dead, but he just wouldn't shut up. So, I was ordered to take him out. But it doesn't make me happy, if that's what you're wondering."

"Ordered, by whom?" Cane shouted. "What did you do when you were outside? Tell me he's wrong, Abell. Tell me you didn't shoot anyone out there!" As he continued to shout at his partner, Cane noticed an opaque film slide vertically across Abell's eyes, like a pair of light blue doors.

"I'm really sorry, cowboy. I really do like you. And I have nothing against the people on this planet, certainly not against the seven people in the office I had to eliminate before I came in here. I really wish they had simply gone home at a decent time. But orders are orders."

"What are you talking about?!" Cane shouted, tightening his grip on his weapon.

"Look, if it makes you feel any better, Jed was one of the seven I killed. Poor unlucky bastard had just come back for his damn golf clubs, so I had to put one right through his forehead. I know you never liked him, but I didn't have anything personal against him. What is it they always say in those gangster movies you like so much? *It wasn't personal; it was just business.'* It was just a matter of tying up loose ends."

In stunned silence, Cane just stared at his partner, his gun hand shaking violently.

"But, I'm certain to get reassigned somewhere else now; and before I do, I have some more loose ends to tie up. Which means that I now have to go home and deal with Felicity and those three awful children of hers . . . *ours*. That one is personal, though; I'm actually looking forward to getting rid of those annoying parasites."

Cane continued to stare at his partner, too shocked to process what he was saying and what he had just done.

"Speaking of loose ends, that unfortunately includes you, too, cowboy."

As Abell raised his weapon, Cane's instincts took over, and he fired.

But nothing happened.

Cane fired again . . . and again.

Still nothing.

Cane looked at his weapon in disbelief.

"Sorry partner," Abell said. "I told you that I thought the firing pin on your piece was defective, but you didn't believe me. Maybe if you had gone to the range once in a while like we're supposed to, you would have discovered that. Fortunately for me, you were always too busy trying to find your next sexual conquest to actually do your job." Then, raising his own weapon, he said, "See you, Cowboy," and fired two shots into Cane's chest.

As the huge man fell to the floor, Abell stepped over him to see if he was wearing a bulletproof vest.

He was not, but Abell wasn't taking any more chances. He put two additional rounds though his former partner's forehead and then calmly stepped out of the interrogation room saying, *"Zwei Fliegen mit einer Klappe schlagen."*

As he made his way past seven other fresh corpses strewn about the office, and as he prepared to head home to eliminate the only other people who might possibly blow his cover, Abell got out the same cellphone he had used earlier to call his direct superiors.

This time he rang home.

"Hi, sweetie. Yeah, really long day, but I'm on my way home right now. Yeah . . . how about you?"

A brief pause.

"Okay, and how about the girls? How are they today?"

Abell paused again as his wife answered. "Really? All three are going to be home tonight? Wow—that is a . . . treat."

A brief pause.

"I know. I'm just unusually excited. All four of my girls are going to be in the same place at the same time . . . and I have a huge surprise for all of you."

A final pause.

"Is it *to die for*? Yeah, I guess you could say that. You might even say, it's *out of this world*. Yep, I love you, too. See you soon."

As he hung up, Abell smiled and began to make his way out towards the "Beige Bitch".

As he did, he began to sing: "*Monday, Monday: Can't trust that day. Monday, Monday: Sometimes it just turns out that way.*"

AUTHOR'S NOTE

The first person to read any of this book was my eighty-five-year-old father. Upon reading the first two chapters, he texted me the following: "Reading some of your next book. Holy crap, you're going after everyone. Do you have a death wish, or did someone shit in your mess kit?"

In response to my father, who feared that this book would result in a series of assassination attempts against me, I offer by way of explanation (but certainly not apology) the end of a letter written by Josiah Quincy, Jr. to his father who, in 1770, was dismayed to learn that his son had undertaken the defense of the hated British soldiers who had allegedly shot eleven colonists in Boston, killing five of them.

> *"I never harboured the expectation, nor any great desire, that all men should speak well of me. To inquire my duty, and to do it, is my aim. Being mortal, I am subject to error; and conscious of this, I wish to be diffident. Being a rational creature, I judge for myself, according to the light afforded me. When a plan of conduct is formed with an honest deliberation, neither murmuring, slander, nor reproaches move. For my single self, I consider, judge, and with reason hope to be immutable. There are honest men in all sects, I wish their approbation; there are wicked bigots in all parties, I abhor them.*
>
> *I am, truly and affectionately, your Son,*
> *Josiah Quincy, Jr."*

Let me put it to you another way, dad. I didn't set out to deliberately piss anybody off. But, sometimes, you just have to call 'em like you see 'em.

I am, truly and affectionately, your Son,
Stephen A. Reger

9 7 9 8 3 3 0 4 4 2 6 2 1